ALAN E. SAMUEL received his Ph.D. from Yale University, where he is now Assistant Professor of Classics. He has written a book dealing with the chronology of Egypt under the Ptolemies and many articles dealing with ancient history. He has recently travelled widely in Egypt and Greece, visiting sites and taking photographs. Mr. Samuel is secretary of the American Society of Papyrologists.

MAP I

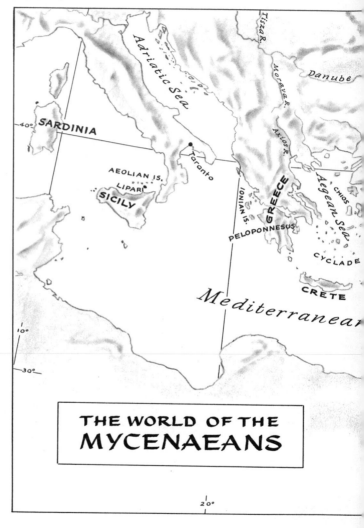

THE WORLD OF THE
MYCENAEANS

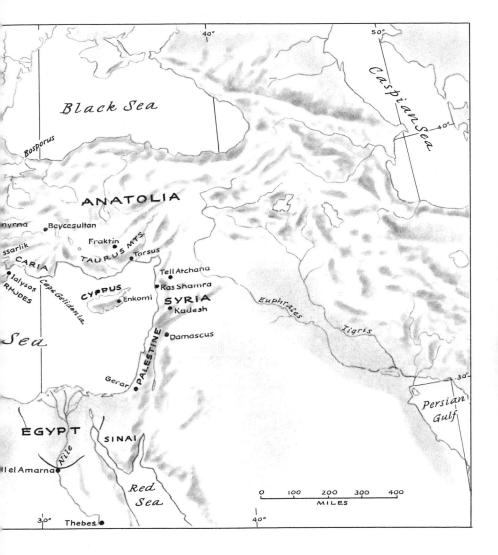

Black Sea

Bosporus

ANATOLIA

myrna • Beycesultan

• Fraktin

ssarlik   TAURUS MTS.

• CARIA   • Tarsus

• Ialysos   Cape Gelidonia

RHODES   CYPRUS   • Tell Atchana

• Enkomi   • Ras Shamra

SYRIA

• Kadesh

Sea   • Damascus

PALESTINE

Gerar

EGYPT   SINAI

Nile

l el Amarna•

Red
Sea

3|0°   • Thebes

Caspian Sea

Euphrates

Tigris

Persian
Gulf

```
   0    100   200   300   400
   |_____|_____|_____|_____|
           MILES
```

40°   50°

40°

30°

40°

The Mycenaeans in History

ALAN E. SAMUEL

The Mycenaeans In History

PRENTICE-HALL, INC. *Englewood Cliffs, N.J.*

A SPECTRUM BOOK

To my wife
in allusion to all that I have said in private

Preface

LIKE NATURE, ARCHAEOLOGISTS AND HISTORIANS ABHOR A VAC-
uum. When this book was begun there existed no general account of the Greek Bronze Age, nor was there any survey of
what was known about Mycenaean civilization. Now there are
several excellent books, and a reader can easily find connected
and full accounts of archaeological discoveries and more than
enough contemporary interpretations of the finds.

Certainly another book is hardly needed unless it is quite
different. Another book should do more than express a natural
reluctance to strangle one's child before the world even sees it.
It seems to me that after the publication of *Greece in the
Bronze Age* by Emily Vermeule, the author of yet another book
should explain just what it is that he expects to add. I propose
to do that in this preface.

I should say at the outset that I am not a specialist in prehistoric Greek archaeology, or indeed, even an archaeologist. I approach the material found and discussed by archaeologists from
the point of view of an historian. Thus I do not give a comprehensive account of the major finds or report all the work of the
field archaeologists, but rather try to find out and to tell what
early Greek society was like, how it grew, and what happened
to it. If there is information of an archaeological nature in the
book, it owes its appearance to the fact that all the evidence
now available is archaeological.

This then, is the major difference between this book and others on the same subject. This book, I hope, is primarily a history. I have tried to place in these chapters information interesting and useful to the historian of antiquity, and to the stu-

dent of ancient culture in general. I have tried to push the writing of Greek history, *qua* history, back to the beginnings of settlement on the Greek mainland. My main concern has been to show to those interested in classical civilization the major developments and the kinds of societies which preceded the Hellenic.

Even when so much remains to be learned, there is far too much material at hand for all of it to be brought usefully to bear on the interpretation of early Greek history. A great deal has been omitted here, and though I have often used details to illustrate, to explain, and sometimes to defend an argument, much that is important and interesting did not find its way into these pages.

An entire corpus of literature has deliberately been set aside. No one who thinks of Mycenaean civilization can avoid also thinking of Homer and the Trojan War. The *Iliad* first set Heinrich Schliemann to work to discover the sites of the cities of which Homer sang and no historian or archaeologist since has been able to avoid a comparison between the materials found and the words of the poet. I have tried to avoid this in writing, at least. Certainly there is a great deal of agreement today about the nature of the Homeric poems. We agree that they were recited orally, perhaps for hundreds of years, before they were written down. This means that although the poems sing of Mycenaean times, and perhaps even have Mycenaean origins, there was almost infinite opportunity for change, both in major and minor details. Although some words, lines, or even sections refer to the Bronze Age, others arise from a society much later in time. Even the language is no secure indication of the historical accuracy of a section; some sections which certainly refer to the Bronze Age were, linguistically speaking, composed quite late.

It is impossible to determine from internal evidence which information in the poetry deals with the Bronze Age and which is later. An oral tradition is whimsical and unreliable in the preservation of its history. When we identify Bronze Age references in the poems, we do so from archaeology, not from the poems themselves, and even these identifications change as we excavate more. When we find that Homer has preserved an accurate recollection of the Bronze Age, we do so by producing independent evidence from a Bronze Age site. Without the excavated material the Homeric reference would be speculative and unconfirmed, useless for history. What we know, we know from excavation.

Thus, Homer provides no real evidence for history. We see none of the bureaucratic administration to which the Linear B tablets attest, and much of the artistic and architectural grandeur of Mycenaean society is missing from his verses. It would be dangerous indeed to use any unconfirmed statement in Homer as evidence for the nature of Mycenaean civilization; conversely, with the evidence from excavation, we do not need Homer. Thus, questions about the date and purpose of the Trojan War, the political organization of Greece, or the relations between the great Greek kings who appear in the *Iliad* will eventually be resolved by archaeologists and historians. The poems alone can tell us no more than they did before Schliemann turned his first shovelful of earth. Homer belongs to literature, not to history.

There is a great deal more in Greek tradition than Homer to be set aside. Although we do not hear so often of the information in the later Greek literary tradition, much in Greek drama refers to the same period as did Homer. No historian has felt compunction at dismissing this evidence, and the reasons for this are essentially the same as those which disqualify Homer's. There is also information about the Bronze Age in the works of the ancient Greek historians, and although some of this has proved accurate, some has turned out to be wrong, and a great deal remains untested or unprovable. This information too was filtered through the oral tradition and cannot be accepted without the confirmation which makes it unnecessary. This is even more true of the work of the late Greek chronographers, who tried to put the accounts of poets and historians in some kind of rational and chronological order. Their success often may have been gained at the expense of accuracy. Though their works, if right, could give us a date for the fall of Mycenaean civilization or the Trojan War (if it was fought), we have yet no test for their accuracy. Anyway, they conflict.

The safest course is to set aside all information which is inherently unreliable. This means that our account will be somewhat limited, depending as it does on the archaeological evidence, which presents the only available information contemporary with Mycenaean civilization. This does not mean that the account will necessarily be right. Even when we use only Mycenaean evidence, we must interpret it, and there are myriad opportunities to go wrong. Each interpretation will find new mistakes to make. Even what may be right in our terms may prove irrelevant in the future; as each generation approaches history it asks different questions and finds different problems.

As I finish this book, I am conscious of a great debt to Professor Emily Vermeule, not so much for helping me as for helping all of us. Her recently published *Greece in the Bronze Age* establishes a basis for all future study of early Greece. Her comprehensive chapters on various aspects of Mycenaean archaeology and her full bibliography have saved me, and will save others, much work. I should hope that any whose interests have been piqued by this history would turn next to her book.

I also owe much to Professor Ann L. Perkins for her teaching and for her direct help with this book. Much that is good in these pages comes from her; the mistakes are my own contribution to Aegean prehistory. I am also in the debt of Professor Emmett L. Bennett, Jr., who first introduced me to and patiently tried to teach me to use the Linear B tablets. So too I thank Professor C. Bradford Welles, who patiently read and reread drafts of the manuscript to help me to produce a rational history. Finally, Miss Francesca Tillona and Mr. Walter Langsam were most patient and helpful in suggesting useful changes, and in preparing the final manuscript for the press.

A. E. S.

Contents

Illustrations

The Mycenaeans in History

MAINLAND GREECE

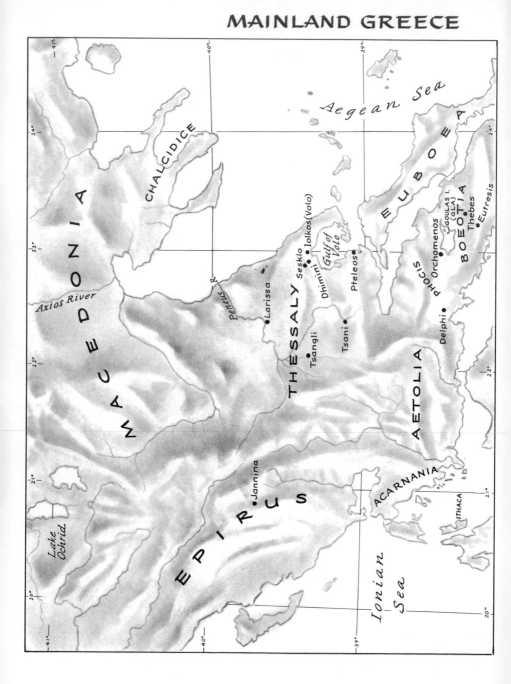

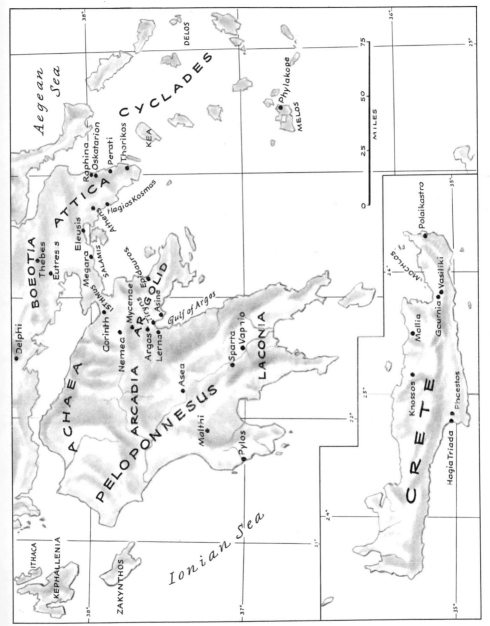

Introduction

THE TERMS "MYCENAEANS" AND "MYCENEAN," TAKEN VERY
strictly, should refer only to the inhabitants of the city of Mycenae and their culture. But, because Mycenae was the first
Bronze Age site identified in Greece, it has been used as a reference point, and thus the words have been used often by archaeologists and historians to refer to the people and civilization of Greece in the Late Bronze Age. This may be careless
language, but it is understood, and it is probably too late now
to go back to a purer terminology. At any rate, in this book,
Mycenaeans are the inhabitants of Greece in the Late Bronze
Age, and the adjective *Mycenaean* refers to their culture as a
whole or to aspects of it.

This book, and others like it, show the tendency of history to
expand at both ends. While we today make history for our children to study, some of our scholars push our knowledge of the
past farther and farther back, so that there is always more to
learn. One hundred years ago, Greek history could have begun
with the traditional date of the first celebration of the Olympic
Games in 776 B.C. The earliest events in that history were only
very imperfectly known, and the historian could give a connected account and feel somewhat sure of his facts only when
he reached the great wars and the flowering of culture of the
fifth century B.C. Even today there are great gaps in our knowledge of the first four centuries of the first millennium B.C., and
historians disagree by as much as a hundred years in the dating
of major wars.

Today there is a whole new epoch of Greek history, not even
guessed at a hundred years ago. When we think of the genius of

Greek civilization, we think of the great writers of plays, Aeschylus, Sophocles, and Euripides, of the philosophy of Plato and Aristotle, of Herodotus and Thucydides who gave us the histories of their own times. But this view of the Greek accomplishment is a limited one. Although the culture which these writers represent is the very foundation of our own civilization, it was not the only contribution of the Greeks. That famous Greek civilization, with its literature, art, and political history, was the second cultural accomplishment of the Greeks, and perhaps should be called Hellenic, as the Greeks would have called it, to distinguish it from the flowering of society which preceded it. That predecessor was the Mycenaean civilization.

Our knowledge of this great culture is still severely limited. We have no books of history to tell of the wars the Mycenaeans fought, of the failures they experienced or the successes that brought them to prominence in the Mediterranean. No records remain to establish a chronology of dynasties or leaders for even one Mycenaean city, or to show clearly what the relations were between the cities. We do not have their literature, by which we might better understand them. We know nothing of their philosophy, and almost nothing of the religion they lived by. What remains is their art; we have some paintings, a few pieces of sculpture, the foundations of several buildings, and some of their masterworks of ceramic art. Besides this, we have a tiny percentage of what they wrote, and of that only business records survive. Still, with this little we can see how great they were.

The ancestors of the Mycenaeans came to Greece at least as early as 2000 B.C., and they may have been there long before. Men have been in Greece since Neanderthal times, as early as 70,000 B.C., and by about 6000 B.C. there were settled Neolithic communities. For three thousand years after that the country was developed; new people came in from time to time; and thriving Stone Age cultures grew and died. In the third millennium B.C. the use of bronze was introduced, and for the first stage of Bronze Age civilization—a period of about one thousand years, called the Early Helladic Period—the new technology brought a high level of prosperity to many towns in Greece.

I. The Argive plain
from the citadel of
Tiryns.

We do not know who the Stone Age settlers and first Bronze Age inhabitants were. We have no knowledge of their ethnic stock or of the language or languages they spoke. The changes brought to Greece over these four thousand years suggest new cultural impulses arriving from time to time, and these may have had their sources in successive arrivals of peoples of different origins. Some of these peoples might have been the remote ancestors of the Mycenaeans; it is also possible that there was no kinship at all between the early inhabitants of Greece and later arrivals. In any case, it is certain that the fore-bears of the Mycenaeans were in Greece by the end of the third millennium B.C. From 2200 to 1900 a series of destructions

3

smashed town after town and overturned the prosperous Early Helladic society. If the Early Helladic peoples bore no relation to the Mycenaeans, the men responsible for these disasters did. From the end of the Early Helladic Period (2200-1900 B.C.) on, the history of Greece in the Middle Bronze Age is one of steady build-up of civilization to reach that pinnacle of culture which we call Mycenaean. There is no break from the beginning of the Middle Bronze Age to the end of Mycenaean civilization itself.

This growing civilization was truly Mycenaean by the middle of the sixteenth century B.C. By then great wealth existed in Greece, and soon after, if not already, palaces and walled citadels rose above towns which had long been settled in important strategic and commercial locations. In the succeeding four hundred years, scores of small and large towns flourished in even the remotest parts of Greece. The remains of many towns show that major works of architecture and large-scale engineering projects were conceived and carried to completion. The later Greeks, the Hellenes, were so staggered by the traces of Mycenaean masonry that they assumed that the walls must have been built by semidivine giants, the Cyclopes, and the term *Cyclopaean* survives today to denote the Mycenaean method of building walls with monumental blocks of stone. These walls, parts of which still stand, point to the centers of power all through Greece. At Mycenae, at nearby Tiryns, at Pylos on the west coast of the Peloponnesus, at Thebes in Boeotia, and at Iolkos in Thessaly the Mycenaeans settled and built communities. It seems, from what we know today, that the Mycenaeans established towns in all the places which were to be significant for one reason or another in the later classical period, and in many others besides. In Mycenaean times Greece was probably as heavily settled and prosperous as it ever was to be again, and the general level of culture may have been far higher than the silent stones would ever lead us to assume.

The palaces were decorated by magnificent frescoes of great artistic and technical quality, and in centers throughout Greece the Mycenaeans knew and used the art of writing. The decipherment of this writing, a syllabic script called Linear B, shows that the language was an early dialect of Greece; inasmuch as this script and language were used wherever there was writing in Greece, it seems certain that the Mycenaeans were Greek. That is, they were Greek in the same sense that the classical Greeks called all people Hellenic (Greek) who spoke Greek.

The Mycenaeans had more than language in common with their descendants. Like the classical Hellenes, they were a commercial people. The few remaining records suggest a thriving and complex economy, and an elaborate bureaucracy built to administer agriculture and trade. Commerce was so heavy within Greece itself that regional differences in art and writing seem to have been virtually eliminated, although nothing indicates actual political union of the scattered towns and cities. The Mycenaeans, like later Greeks, crossed the Mediterranean and reached Italy, Palestine, and Egypt. They planted colonies or trading settlements in some eastern centers, and probably dominated Mediterranean commerce for three or four hundred years. Some Mycenaeans were important and powerful enough to be reckoned with by the Egyptians and Hittites, the most powerful empires of the East.

This great accomplishment was not to last. In the waning decades of the thirteenth century palace after palace was attacked. Some towns were not completely destroyed, and managed to resurrect some of the grandeur of the civilization of the preceding centuries even after the terrible disruption which had been visited upon the Mycenaean world. But the recovery was temporary. By 1100 B.C. another wave of destruction overwhelmed almost all the remaining centers and swept away the Mycenaean civilization.

We do not know who the destroyers were, or why they attacked the Mycenaeans. They left no clues to their existence but the destruction they wrought. Modern historians have called this the Dorian invasion, to explain the Doric and other Greek dialects in classical times, but this theory of Dorian invasion just puts into modern terms the Hellenic recollection of the "return of the sons of Heracles" into the Peloponnesus, and certainly does not fit what we know of those turbulent times. The truth is that although we know that Mycenaean culture was brought to a disastrous close, we know neither the agents nor the reasons.

Though the centers of Mycenaean civilization were destroyed, Mycenaean culture left its imprint on the later Hellenes. Entirely apart from the literary and religious recollections of later Greeks, many real survivals of Mycenaean civilization can be found in Greek classical culture. Many "Hellenic" gods were first worshipped in Mycenaean times. Some towns were not destroyed, and there the slow recovery and development into classical culture proceeded directly from Mycenaean traditions.

Along with much that was new in Hellenic culture, there was a great deal derived from the first flowering of Greek genius. Great cultural achievements do not die easily. The thousand years of the growth of Mycenaean civilization have not been lost completely. Our own culture is built, in a sense, on that of the classical world, and we do not consider the work of the Hellenes and the Romans lost. So too, the later Greeks benefited from the achievements of the Mycenaeans. It may even be that the Mycenaeans did more than just contribute to the Hellenic accomplishment; the Mycenaeans, with their commercial enterprise, their explorations of the Mediterranean, their settlement of cities, their art and now lost literature, may have made classical civilization possible.

CHAPTER ONE

The Discovery
of Mycenaean Civilization

ALONG THE PASS FROM CORINTH TO ARGOS, ABOUT FIFTEEN
miles south of Corinth, lies the acropolis of Mycenae, nestled in
the hills above the plain of Argos. The site was mentioned by
that ancient tourist, Pausanias, who had seen in the second century A.D. the great city wall, the Lion Gate, and some tombs
which he attributed to the Homeric heroes. For almost two
thousand years after that, however, the site lay unexplored, visited only by an occasional tourist, while the attention of the
world focused upon Athens, the center of Greek culture in clas
sical and Roman times.

But at the end of the nineteenth century men were to look
more closely at Mycenae. The art of archaeology, which had
been primarily a scholarly treasure hunt, became an organized
and scientific search for knowledge. Instead of digging at random for precious objects of art, archaeologists excavated wide
areas, and, to be sure that all finds could be studied properly,
they excavated stratum by stratum, so that the relative ages of
the objects would be known. This century has seen elaborate
refinements of field work; the locations of all objects are recorded, and almost everything found is photographed in place
before being removed. The archaeologist can now hope to re-
construct the material aspect of the people whose town he is
excavating. The chronology established by the various strata
enables him to trace changes in architectural styles, and the
evolution of the techniques of pottery-making and painting reveals the artistic development of the culture. Radical stylistic

7

breaks suggest the arrival of new people, and the "burned levels" found in so many excavations are evidence of destructions visited on the sites.

The Excavation of Mycenae

The founder of modern archaeology was Heinrich Schliemann, whose intuition and devotion to the truth of Homer's *Iliad* had brought him in 1873 to the excavation of a great city near Hissarlik, Turkey. This he identified as Troy. Although Schliemann's city was actually five hundred years older than Homer's Troy, he had discovered the site of Troy and had proved the existence of a great civilization antedating the culture and cities of Hellenic Greece.

In 1876 Schliemann turned his attention to Mycenae, and by spring he had cleared an area near the Lion Gate northwest of the citadel. This area was circular, and surrounded by a double row of huge slabs. At first Schliemann believed it to have been the assembly place for the city. However, there were within the circle a number of graves, simple shafts sunk into the rock. By the fall of the year Schliemann had excavated five of the graves, bringing to light one of the most magnificent treasures ever found by an archaeologist—a marvelous array of gold and silver cups and goblets, death masks and clothing ornaments, vases of clay and stone, and beautifully inlaid bronze daggers and swords. The gold alone weighed over eighty pounds.

The importance of Schliemann's discovery was clear. A great civilization, long antedating that of classical Greece, had existed in the Greek lands. Much more was to come. In 1884 Schliemann turned to the excavation of Tiryns, a citadel about ten miles to the south, situated on a jutting rock overlooking the plain of Argos not far from the sea. He had stopped at Tiryns briefly in 1876 and later had attempted excavations at Orchomenos in Boeotia, but he had found only a domed tomb, which he cleared, bringing to light the remains of a decorated ceiling. In 1882 he was joined by William Dörpfeld, and the two worked together at Tiryns. In that year and the next, they cleared the first great palace found in Greece. Schliemann had already examined briefly the walls on the citadel of Tiryns. These walls, which average fifty feet in height, are as much as forty feet thick in some places; great stretches are hollow, with galleries topped by pointed arches running along inside the masonry. Dörpfeld and Schliemann now proceeded to clear part of the acropolis itself, revealing a palace of very complicated plan.

This discovery was to be Schliemann's last. In succeeding years he conducted new searches (notably one for the palace of the legendary King Minos of Crete), but with no success. Nevertheless, he had opened a new world for archaeologists and historians. He had proved that a rich and powerful civilization

II. Grave Circle A at Mycenae.

III. An air view of Tiryns.

—advanced in architecture, metal-working, and art—had existed in Greece long before classical times.

Crete and the Minoans

Although Schliemann had not found the palace of Minos, another archaeologist proved that he had been right to search. In 1893 Sir Arthur Evans, while investigating the evidence of a culture which had existed on the island of Crete, discovered the first evidence that the preclassical civilization of that island had been literate. Some stones had been found bearing a mysterious hieroglyphic writing. There was also what Evans called a "linear" script. In 1895 Evans' discovery of an offering table engraved in the linear script led him to assume that the art of writing had been known on Crete as early as 1500 B.C., if not before. The extent of literacy was not known, however, until Evans' excavation of the great palace at Knossos in 1900.

This was the palace of Minos, for which Schliemann had searched in vain. The excavations directed by Evans were carried on over a number of years, gradually baring an extensive palace of complex plan. A large central court was surrounded by an intricate maze of rooms, and staircases show that some parts of the palace were at least two stories high. There are the remains of an elaborate and ingenious water-supply system. The walls of the rooms were covered with magnificent frescoes of men, women, buildings, and imaginary animals. Within the palace Evans found a hoard of clay tablets inscribed in linear script, clear evidence that there had not only been literacy, but an extensive use of writing.

The discoveries at Knossos were arousing the interest of the whole world, and the newspapers and magazines of the day were filled with pictures and articles about Evans' work. Other archaeologists were busy elsewhere on Crete. At Phaestos, south of Knossos, Federigo Halbherr found another palace; a short distance away, near a small church named Hagia Triada, he found still another, though smaller, one. While these discoveries were being made, at the eastern tip of the island, at Palaikastro, a whole town was found, some strata of which were contemporary with Knossos; elsewhere in eastern Crete two more towns were found.

It was clear by 1910 that an extraordinarily rich and powerful civilization had existed on Crete long before the flowering of Hellenic culture. Egyptian objects found on Crete made it possible to date the different periods of the Minoan civilization, as the newly discovered culture was called. Evans had delineated three phases: Early Minoan (ca. 3000-2100 B.C.), Middle Minoan (ca. 2100-1600), and Late Minoan (ca. 1600-1100). Evans' work showed that in the Late Minoan period, during which the palaces and towns of Crete had reached their highest affluence, two serious disturbances had struck the civilization. The period had begun with the destruction of the palace at Knossos, and Evans hazarded a guess that this had been the result of a revolution. In 1400 B.C. another catastrophe had overtaken the island: the palace at Hagia Triada was destroyed, and soon after that the palaces at Phaestos and Knossos were laid waste. Evans thought that this later devastation occurred at the hands of the mainlanders, whom he believed to have been under the domination of the Minoans until that time.

The Exploration of Greece

Meanwhile, investigation of the mainland sites continued. In 1886 Schliemann's successor in the excavation of Mycenae, Chrestos Tsountas, discovered the palace on the acropolis. This building, unlike those of Tiryns and Knossos, is small and relatively simple in conception. Evidence of Mycenaean occupation elsewhere in Greece now began to come to light. It was discovered that Attica had been inhabited: in 1886 some tombs were excavated near Athens and pieces of Mycenaean pottery were recognized. To the south, in Vaphio of Laconia, a rich grave was opened, yielding two beautifully worked gold cups—the famous "Vaphio" cups which lent their name to the type: short cups with no stem, and a small handle near the top.

Mycenaean remains also appeared in the north of Greece. Tombs were opened at Dhimini in Thessaly in 1886, and near Thessalian Larissa a few years later. In 1912 Alan J. B. Wace and Maurice Thompson published the results of their survey of Thessaly. Sixteen sites could be identified either by tombs or pieces of pottery or ruins—three were in Phocis and four in Boeotia, in addition to the well-known Orchomenos, Thebes, and Goulas Island.

On the island of Aegina, in the gulf near Athens, a Mycenaean treasure of gold cups and ornaments had been found (which Tsountas argued had been deposited after the close of the Mycenaean era) and some pottery as well. On the island of Salamis, just across from Athens, excavated graves revealed pottery from the very end of the Mycenaean period.

Outside Greece itself, new discoveries proved the extent of the influence of the Aegean civilizations. From Enkomi in east-

IV. The Vaphio cup.

crn Cyprus came a treasure of gold and silver almost as rich as
that from Mycenae itself, and more than twenty-five sites were
found in the northeastern part of the island. Among the Cycladic Islands in the southern Aegean the excavations at Phylakope in Melos produced evidence of Mycenaean settlement or
trade. Cretan pottery had been found in Egypt in 1887; two
years later Sir Flinders Petrie found pieces of more than eight
hundred mainland vases at Tel-el Amarna, the capital city of
Akhnaton, who ruled Egypt from 1379 to 1362 B.C.

It was clear that a great people had lived in Greece and
Crete. They had left traces throughout Greece and even beyond the Aegean. Because the most impressive finds had been
made on Crete, it was natural that that island should have been
considered the focus of Aegean life. Despite the very rich discovery at Mycenae, the excavations which Evans was con-
ducting on Crete at the beginning of the twentieth century
were of paramount interest. As he and his colleagues revealed

13

the successive strata of centuries of habitation at Knossos and the other Cretan sites, it seemed only logical to conclude that the island civilization had provided the impetus for the mainland culture. It is difficult now to appreciate the excitement generated by Evans' discoveries. The world was astounded to find that people on Crete had acquired the art of writing 1500 years before the birth of Christ, and had learned the principles of plumbing and were piping running water into dwellings. Not only the excavator was convinced of the importance of Crete; scholars all over the world joined him in raising the Cretan kingdom to the leadership of the whole Greek world. Evidence such as the hoard of mainland Mycenaean vases found in Egypt, which might have created doubt, was explained by attributing to Crete a worldwide commerce which transported goods from the mainland all over the Mediterranean.

By the time World War I closed in on the nations of Europe, most scholars had assessed the discoveries of the preceding fifty years. H. R. Hall, in *Aegean Archaeology* (1915), provides one interpretation of the first years of discovery:

The most important remains of ancient Aegean civilization have been found on the island of Crete, and there the whole story of this civilization can be studied from its beginning to its end. Crete was the main focus of the Aegean culture. It came to the mainland of Greece from Crete, and in Greece was really, if not exactly a foreign, at any rate a nonindigenous culture.

Between the Wars

After the war archaeologists returned to the field to continue their search for knowledge of the mainland culture. The way had been prepared by American archaeologists, led by Carl Blegen, at an excavation at Korakou near Corinth in 1915 and 1916. The publication of their findings in 1921 provided evidence from a carefully excavated site, and Blegen was the first to give the mainland culture some credit for creativity and development independent of Crete. In 1921 and 1922 Blegen continued his investigations, excavating a site on the hill of Zygouries, in an upland valley about halfway between Corinth and Mycenae. No rich finds were made, but the architectural remains and the pottery and other implements found in the houses and tombs proved invaluable in reconstructing the histories of these towns, which had existed for two millennia and had died over three thousand years ago.

Investigation was proceeding in Attica, Boeotia, Thessaly, Macedonia, and in Chalcidice, the three-pronged peninsula which juts out from the Macedonian coastline. Excavations were carried out during the 1920s and 1930s and, by the time that World War II broke out, thirty sites with Mycenaean remains had been discovered.

None of these excavations, however, had produced rich and exciting new finds. Very little precious metal, exotic pottery, or striking architecture had been uncovered during this entire period. So, although the intensive investigation of Greece had pointed out the strong influence of the South on the rest of Greece, and though there was even evidence of some mainland influence on Crete during the Late Helladic II Period, the attention of the world and of archaeologists was not caught as it had been by the excavation of Knossos. The magnificent palace at Knossos, with its many rooms, beautiful frescoes, and—above all—its evidence of writing, still stood as the great proof that the Aegean culture had emanated from Crete. Even though more material had been excavated by Wace at Mycenae, and although excavation in Laconia had brought forth evidence of settlement in more than two dozen places, the focus of world attention was still the achievement of Crete. In spite of the evidence from the western shore of the Mediterranean and the discovery of pottery along the Palestinian coast pointing to an extremely influential mainland Greek culture, the Minoan culture of Crete was still regarded as the most pervasive.

In 1939, after a long and productive expedition to Troy, Carl Blegen returned to Greece. During a reconnaissance of the southwestern coast of the country, about six miles north of classical Pylos, he discovered the site of a Mycenaean palace. Blegen set to work testing the site with trial trenches, and from one of these came more than six hundred complete or fragmentary clay tablets, bearing the Linear B script identified at Knossos. By a stroke of incredibly good luck, Blegen had hit upon the archive room of the palace. There was now evidence of writing on the mainland, even though some scholars maintained that the mainlanders had learned the art of writing from the Cretans or had stolen the tablets during an attack on Knossos.

This was the state of knowledge of early Greece immediately prior to World War II. Many strides had been made during the preceding twenty-five years and much had been learned about the great pre-Hellenic civilizations of Greece and Crete.

With the return of peace, the archaeologists were able to resume their work. A new era was dawning. The last of the great early excavators, Arthur Evans, had died in 1941. The British archaeologist Wace made further excavations at Mycenae, and found tablets similar to those Blegen had discovered at Pylos in 1939. Blegen returned to Pylos in 1952 and began excavation of the palace. Work is still continuing there. Much of the palace is now cleared, and although the palace is apparently smaller than that of Knossos, it is nevertheless an extensive structure.

Elsewhere in Greece the postwar years have brought more information about the extent of Mycenaean settlement. A number of sites were discovered in the northwestern part of the Peloponnesus, in the plain of Achaea and up in the hills. Tombs, and in some cases whole cemeteries, were found, and traces of a settlement were located in the hills in 1956. The clay tablets found at Mycenae came from the private houses excavated during this period. Many more Mycenaean tombs were excavated in Attica, and a very important Mycenaean cemetery was found at Perati, on the western coast. At Athens itself, a Mycenaean staircase and well have been found on the north slope of the Acropolis, and Mycenaean burials are coming to light in the town below.

On the isthmus—the narrow strip connecting the Peloponnese with the rest of Greece—a Mycenaean wall has been discovered, cutting off the Peloponnese from the north. In Boeotia, the enormous citadel on Goulas Island (Gla) is currently being excavated. At Delphi a Mycenaean level has been discovered. More Mycenaean sites have been found in Thessaly, and the palace walls found at Volo, the site of ancient Iolkos, on the shore at the northern end of the Gulf of Volo, indicate an important center of Mycenaean power and influence in Thessaly. Indeed, there is evidence that Mycenaean influence extended even into the mountains in Epirus, in northwestern Greece; Late Helladic tombs and pieces of pottery were found at Jannina.

Investigation and discovery have also continued outside Greece. The extraordinary wealth and power of the Cretan civilization have received additional confirmation as chance finds revealed more tombs, settlements, and houses on that island. A Mycenaean settlement was found on Chios, and Mycenaean building levels were discovered on Delos. Major finds are made each season of the current excavations of Kea. Little was done on Rhodes to add to the knowledge of the Mycenaean settlement there gained in prewar investigations, but pieces of Mycenaean pottery were found at Smyrna, on the western coast of Turkey. From Beycesultan, in the Turkish interior, came a few pieces of Mycenaean pottery and some stone pommels of Mycenaean type swords and daggers, indicating that Mycenaean trade, probably using Rhodes as a base, had penetrated far inland. A single vase found at a Hittite site, at Fraktin, far to the east in Turkey, indicated that Mycenaean trade came into that part of Turkey from Tarsus, a port at the northeastern corner of the Mediterranean. Excavations continued on Cyprus at Enkomi, which had yielded rich Mycenaean material in the past, and Mycenaean pottery was found in some Late Bronze Age buildings there.

There will be important new finds from current excavations, and there is no doubt that there will be great discoveries in sites not yet even known. The historian will revise his concept of Mycenaean civilization as more material comes to light, and will change his mind again as archaeology gives him new evidence. We do not yet know enough to be sure that even our broad generalizations about the Mycenaeans will be regarded as valid ten years hence. Still, the archaeologists have brought forth enough material to make it possible for the historian to give a connected account of Mycenaean culture.

CHAPTER TWO

The Forerunners of the Mycenaeans

The Neolithic Period

RECENT DISCOVERIES have shown that men lived in Greece as early as Palaeolithic times, some sixty thousand years B.C. The traces of Neanderthal man found are scanty, and we know almost nothing of Old Stone Age culture in Greece. Yet the scant traces we have show that men came into Greece very early, just as they were moving into the other parts of Europe. These first hunters traveled south, and some even came into the Peloponnesus; more evidence may show better what they were like, and how they lived. From the little we know of them now, however, we can see no connection between the first human exploration of the Greek peninsula, and the real exploitation of Greece which was to come scores of thousands of years later.

EARLY NEOLITHIC THESSALY. The earliest evidence of settlement in Greece indicates that men settled in Macedonia, Thessaly, central Greece, the Peloponnesus, and Crete by about 3500 B.C. The most exciting developments took place in Thessaly, where there are two separate but closely related clusters of sites. In the early part of the Neolithic period, a number of unfortified towns were built in central Thessaly, near the modern towns of Sesklo, Tsangli, Tsani, and Zerelia. The lack of any fortification at these sites suggests that the communities lived peacefully with each other, and that there were no wars or threats of war.

Although there seems to have been no organization to the placement of houses, there were narrow alleyways along which people could wend their way through town. The towns must have had a somewhat peculiar appearance, for circular houses are mixed in among the more common rectangular dwellings. There were also differences iń the method of construction; some of the houses were made of mud on a wood and reed framework, while others had walls of sun-dried brick on stone foundations. These more ambitious structures may indicate differences in the owners' economic or social position, just as homes today stand as physical symbols of affluence.

The ceramic techniques of these early inhabitants of Greece were quite advanced, and there are many examples of excellent pottery-making. But far more memorable than even the finest cups and bowls are the innumerable little female figurines found all over Greece and the Balkans. The most common type emphasized woman's generative role: she is portrayed with large protruding breasts and enormous pendulous buttocks. Archaeologists find these figurines so unattractive that they consider them to have played only a religious role, representing female productivity rather than female beauty.

These statuettes, at least one of which does portray woman as modern man would like to think of her, demonstrate clearly

V. Neolithic figurines.

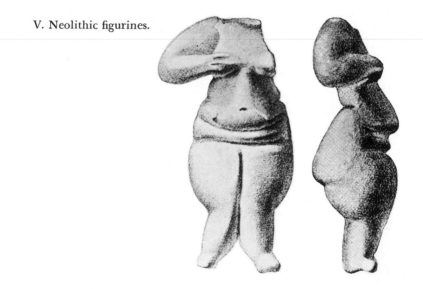

the problem involved in the interpretations of archaeological evidence. An artifact, an object, cannot speak; it cannot tell us its use or significance. All we know is that which we deduce from its mere existence and the situation in which it was found. To this task the historian brings all his knowledge of the particular culture and of related civilizations, but his final conclusions are often affected by his own, often unverbalized, assumptions about human nature. Because we know that primitive men often fashion figures which have significance in totemistic religion, we are inclined to attribute to such figures a religious purpose. In these terms, Neolithic men created the little figures as part of a fertility cult, either as representations of a fertility goddess, or possibly even to serve as surrogates for offerings to such a goddess. At present, this explanation seems the best and we should probably be correct in assuming that the men responsible for these first civilizations in Greece believed that a female deity had a great power over their lives, and that this deity could in some way be influenced by the use of the little figurines. But it is important to remember that this reconstruction of Neolithic religion is based on the interpretation of objects which, though fascinating to the archaeologist who discovered them, never spoke to him, or to the historian, or, in all probability, to the Neolithic men who made them.

The archaeologist has given us more than the figurines to provide insight into life in these communities more than five thousand years ago. As tools take on recognizable appearances, we are able to identify bone tools for sawing, stone tools for scraping and chopping, and implements for digging and hoeing. These artifacts vividly call to mind the sewing, woodworking, and farming activities typical of simple agricultural communities which still exist in parts of the world today.

A contemporary cluster of Neolithic villages formed in the northeastern part of Thessaly, where the Peneus River turns eastward to flow into the sea. Similarities in the pottery discovered show that these communities were closely related to those of central Thessaly; nevertheless, a local style, peculiar to the central plateau, of flame-like patterns painted on a white

VI. Dhimini. The new pottery.

background reveals that even in this relatively homogeneous culture local tastes produced variations in artistic traditions.

THE INVASION OF THESSALY. The peace of this world was broken in the fourth millennium B.C. by an irruption of new peoples. Our knowledge of the changes in prehistoric populations rests completely on the evidence of changes in technology and artistic tradition; although the assumptions are sometimes open to challenge, the changes which took place in Thessaly at about this time are so radical that no explanation but invasion will serve. A new group poured into eastern Thessaly, moving down the valley of the Peneus and settling all the way down to the Gulf of Volo. Some of the old settlements accepted the invaders—whether peaceably or under duress is not known; other old towns were abandoned and new settlements were established by the invaders.

Although central Thessaly and the rest of Greece show no evidence of change, strikingly new phenomena appear in the East. New bold designs are found on pottery: groups of strong parallel lines cut irregularly through the field of design and handsome spirals swirl around the whole. The colors are white on red, black on red, and black on white; at the very end of the period there appears a peculiar, crusted paint used in a manner which has strong affinities with a technique and style of design characteristic of a culture in Hungary. In fact, the whole new complex of design types shows affinities with the northern cultures in Hungary, Rumania, West Russia, and Bulgaria, all of which were familiar with spiral decorations. Indeed, there is good reason to call this area "spiral country." This technique and style seems to have been fully developed in the north by the time it burst into Thessaly, and the introduction of so many new phenomena into Greece all at once almost forces the conclusion that the new people came from the north. The simultaneous appearance of the spiral decoration in Macedonia indicates the route taken by these new people. The people—or, at least, the cultural influences—traveled down the Tisza River in Hungary, across the Danube and down the Morava, and then south along the Axios into Macedonia. There may also have been a route along the coast of the Black Sea, into the Bosporus, and then directly across the Aegean into Thessaly.

The people who came down from the Balkans brought vital new influences into Greece. More was changed in Thessaly than the style of decorating pottery. The towns established by the invaders were unlike those they replaced. A new organization was imposed on the communities. In the center of the town the newcomers placed a building with a *megaron* (a large room with forecourt) surrounded by a wall. Beyond this wall stood other buildings, these too protected by walls. At Dhimini there seem to be a number of rings; these may all be fortification walls, but, as so small an area is involved, some may have served as retaining walls for the buildings behind them. There certainly was some fortification, however, and fortification fits the fact that the new people not only brought in fresh artistic and architectural styles; they also brought in war. We even have some of the weapons: sling bullets of clay, shaped like tiny footballs, have been found all over this part of Thessaly. Perhaps most important of all, the planned nature of the towns shows that the invaders must have had a more sophisticated form of village organization, and the location of the large building in the center of the town suggests that community life was focused on some kind of political or religious leadership. As far as is known, this was all new to Greece.

CENTRAL AND SOUTHERN GREECE. While these exciting new influences were being felt in eastern Thessaly, the rest of Greece continued its development. Early Neolithic strata at sites in central Greece—at Athens and Orchomenos, and in the Peloponnesus at Lerna on the Gulf of Argos and at Asea in the mountains of Arcadia—all yield pottery remains attesting to traditions related to, if not identical with, those of Thessaly. Clearly, the population of Greece was homogeneous at the beginning of the Neolithic period. Although north and south developed distinctive pottery styles and some individual cultural styles, the essential relationship shown by the pottery indicates that the early Neolithic period in Greece was marked by cultural unity. As time went on, however, the differences became stronger. Central Thessaly evolved the "Sesklo flame-ware" style of decoration, while the characteristic ware of the south became pottery painted and decorated with a very flat dull (matte) paint. The radical difference between the two styles signifies that the northern and southern areas had lost touch with each other and were developing independently. The division cannot be explained by the invasions, for these had not yet struck Thessaly. It may be that the original unity was simply the result of an early migration into Greece; as time went on and the immigrants settled permanently into different areas, they lost their original cultural homogeneity.

VII. Sesklo "flame-ware."

The Early Helladic Period:
The Introduction of Bronze

The invasions of Thessaly in the late Neolithic period changed the picture radically. Although the influences were not felt south of Thessaly, great changes were taking place in central Greece and the Peloponnesus, where the appearance of a black ware at sites all over the area indicates the development of a cultural unity. This black ware is not found in Thessaly; it is a hallmark of southern culture which shows that the split between north and south persisted to the end of the Neolithic period. The great change in the south, however, had far less to do with pottery than with the use, at certain sites, of bronze tools. At other sites, the stone implements characteristic of Neolithic sites remained in use. The pottery found proves that the sites using metal tools and those still using stone were contemporaneous, thus providing a fascinating record of the first penetration into Greece of a major new technology.

The new technique was not brought by invaders; it must have come into Greece as a result of trade and cultural interchange. Pottery such as the characteristic dull-painted ware has been found in Syria, and it is likely that the importation of metal work arose from contacts between southern Greece and the East. Almost three thousand years before the birth of Christ men in widely separated parts of the world were in contact with one another, and advances made in one place spread across desert and sea to bring radical changes and technological progress to distant areas. The north, which had not developed the art of metal-working, received new influences pouring into Macedonia and Thessaly, but the south, through its connections with to East, moved into a new age.

CENTRAL AND SOUTHERN GREECE. Once the use of metal was introduced at a few sites in Greece, other centers throughout the Peloponnesus followed suit. The new metal, bronze, and its use ushered in a period of wealth and material advancement. The Early Helladic period, as the Early Bronze Age in Greece is called, had begun in some places early in the third millennium B.C.; within a hundred years, perhaps less, bronze was used throughout Greece. The use of metal brought about a precipitous rise in the level of human culture, and the Early Helladic settlements reveal the exciting evidence of architectural, technological, and artistic progress.

At Eutresis in central Greece the high level of culture is indicated by the fine pottery and tools found in the houses there. The architecture itself is far more sophisticated than that of the Neolithic period. Now, stone foundations are usual, and even the houses built at the very beginning of the Early Helladic period have relatively complex floor plans. Many of the houses are divided into two rooms; in the back room, obviously reserved as a working area, there is a hearth, near which frequently lay pieces of fire-blackened pottery used for cooking. By the middle of the Early Helladic period the doors were swung on pivots, and there are holes in the thresholds into which the pins at the bottoms of the doors had been inserted. By the end of the period there were little paved courts out in front of the houses, and brick columns were used as interior supports. Scattered through the houses are pieces of the glazed pottery typical of the Early Helladic period throughout central and southern Greece, as well as axe blades, gardening tools, and clothing pins—all carefully fashioned from copper and bronze.

A little to the east of Eutresis, in Attica, at a place on the coast called Hagios Kosmas, there are houses similar to those at Eutresis arranged in blocks separated by narrow streets. The whole settlement has been covered by the sea, and through the water one can still see the sparkle of the little pieces of stone and pottery with which the streets were paved. Another site in Attica (at Oskatarion, on the northern coast near Raphina) is organized on the same pattern and shows an attempt at fortification; around the city runs a wall of mud bricks raised on a stone foundation. This site, like Eutresis and Hagios Kosmas, attests to the growing organization of society and the accumulation of wealth which permits the improvement of living conditions.

The prosperity brought by the new metal is found throughout Greece, and the location of some of the sites shows that trade was becoming an important factor in the growth of certain communities. In an upland plateau, along the road from Corinth to Mycenae and near the modern town of Zygouries, a very large settlement has been uncovered. The excavation of this site was one of Blegen's great contributions, for here he found signs of continuous habitation from the Early Helladic period to late Mycenaean times. Everywhere Blegen dug on the hill on which the town was situated, he found Early Helladic walls or streets. Here too the streets were paved with pebbles and pottery, and so much of the litter of civilization was cast into them that the modern observer is almost embarrassed at the details of private life lying before him. Clues to what the people ate are provided by the snail and mussel shells lying in the streets; animal bones, split so the marrow could be eaten, conjure pictures of families gnawing at their food during the evening meal and tossing the garbage out the window to the hazard of the unwary passerby.

Although most of the houses are similar to the two-room pivot-door houses of central Greece, one house at Zygouries reveals a more ambitious plan. A large central room flanked on one side by another large room and on the other by two smaller rooms indicates that the prosperity of the settlement in general resulted in more comfortable living for at least one family.

The prosperity of Zygouries must have been based on trade, and the commerce seems to have been remarkably adventurous. Many objects in the houses are evidence of trade with the Aegean Islands, and some point to communications with Crete. Some of the vases found had clearly been imported from the Aegean, and certain silver and bronze pins found in the tombs are almost identical with those found in the tombs of the Cycladic islands. The wealth hinted at by the use of silver is proved by the presence of gold pendants in the tombs. Greece has little precious metal ore, and any use of gold and silver attests to riches accumulated through commerce and export.

Farther south, at Mycenae, there was an Early Helladic

settlement; and on the flat plain, on the great outcropping that is the isolated rock of Tiryns, the foundation walls of an enormous Early Helladic town are ranged along the top of the citadel, down the side, and onto the plain. Elsewhere in the Argolid, at Lerna on the western shore of the Gulf of Argos, another flourishing settlement shows the vigor of this developing culture. The most significant of the many large buildings (it may even be a palace) is the so-called "House of the Tiles," over thirty-five feet wide and more than seventy-five feet long. The

VIII. Lerna. The "House of Tiles" (under a modern roof).

roof of this house had been made up of hundreds of clay tiles. When the building collapsed, the tiles were dashed to the ground. Left there for millennia, they provide mute testimony of a great advance in construction. The builders at Lerna also applied their architectural skill to fortifications. All around the site runs a double wall which, pierced with gates and mounted with protecting towers, provided security for the dwellers within.

THE NORTH LAGS BEHIND. In northern Greece the advance of culture is less noticeable. In Thessaly, which had cradled so flourishing a Neolithic civilization, habitation fell off; the Early Helladic sites are far fewer than the Neolithic. In Macedonia too there is evidence of a failure to build on the accomplishments of the past. Little architecture has been found anywhere in the north and the Early Helladic pottery is of much poorer quality than the Neolithic. At the beginning of the Early Helladic period four millennia ago, northern Greece apparently slipped into the pattern it was so often to follow in classical times: except for occasional surges, like that experienced by Thessaly in Mycenaean times, the north was to remain backward, regarded as barely Greek by the inhabitants of the south. Not until the great victories of Philip of Macedon and his son Alexander was the north again to show that it could lead Greece.

EARLY HELLADIC CIVILIZATION. The transition from Neolithic civilization to Early Helladic seems to have been a peaceful one throughout Greece. The decline in culture in the north cannot be explained by suggesting that invaders had weakened the flourishing Neolithic centers; there is no evidence of the incursion of new peoples (such as that which had affected Greece in the Late Neolithic period) or of the burning or destruction of any of the towns. The gradual spread of the use of bronze was simply not accompanied by the rapid rise in the material level of civilization in the north as it was in the south. Central and southern Greece, which also entered the new age peacefully, made the new material the basis for a radical improvement in housing, and also entered on a new and far-ranging commercial venture. But the people who did all this must have been essentially the descendants of Neolithic inhabitants. Late Neolithic people at some sites continued to use stone tools, while their contemporaries in other towns had learned to use metal and were making tools of bronze. The pottery of towns and villages throughout the Peloponnesus and central Greece provides no evidence of any upheaval: changes in pottery styles were gradual; there was no sudden alteration in decorative techniques, and each modification had its roots in older styles. The Neolithic cultures were learning new techniques and improving on their own past but, except for the introduction of metal, no radical change took place in their art and no basic disturbance altered their lives.

The peaceful years led to an increase in cultural interchange. Pottery styles, shapes, and decoration were similar in the towns of central Greece and the Peloponnesus. All over the area a hallmark of the period appears; the sauceboat, which first appeared as a tall bowl with a short spout and high foot and later developed into a long, low bowl with a handle at one end and a long spout at the other. Advances in ceramic technology had introduced a new glaze. The greater regularity of the pottery shapes and the characteristic marks of the potter's wheel prove that, by the end of the period, clay was no longer merely shaped roughly by hand. The development of metal techniques all over the Peloponnesus allowed people to work precious metals as prosperity brought these into Greece. As trade with the Aegean Islands and Crete brought wealth into Greece, its impact penetrated well into central Greece and into the uplands of the Peloponnesus. It may be hard to understand how the few inches of wall arduously dug from the ground bespeak power and grandeur. But Lerna, spread broadly and surrounded by walls and towers, and looking imperiously across the Gulf of Argos, must have presented an imposing appearance to traders coming across the plain or arriving in small boats along the shores of the Gulf.

THE DESTRUCTION OF EARLY HELLADIC SETTLEMENTS. This prosperity and grandeur, however, came to a sudden and disastrous end about 2200 or 2100 B.C. Not only at Lerna, but all over the Peloponnesus and central Greece, a series of disasters overtook the towns before the end of the Early Helladic period. Blackened and charred pieces of pottery and other objects are scattered everywhere amid the ruins of smashed buildings and shattered walls. The great "House of the Tiles" at Lerna was razed. Zygouries was burned; there are ashes in the settlement of Hagios Kosmas in Attica; and the whole town of Asea, high in the mountains of Arcadia, was destroyed by flames. A flourishing civilization ended in fire and destruction.

The great change that came over Greece in the latter part of the Early Helladic period indicates that the disasters which overtook the towns were the work of new people battling their way into Greece. Wherever this destruction struck, new elements were introduced. At Lerna, the new settlement after the destruction was totally different from the earlier one; Eutresis, which seems to have been spared destruction for a while, also shows a complete new settlement after the fire. As John Caskey, the excavator of Lerna, has said (in *Hesperia XXXIX* [1960], page 30):

. . . *a foreign invasion created widespread havoc in this region and brought to an end the bright flowering of human society which has left its traces in the material remains of the second Early Helladic period.*

Crete: The Beginning of
Minoan Civilization

On Crete, the Early Minoan period moved peacefully into the Middle Minoan period, although the change in culture was almost revolutionary. From the time of Neolithic culture on the island developments had been gradual, and each successive generation had built on the work of its forebears. The inhabitants of Crete had contact with the Aegean Islands during the Neolithic period and in their architecture (which placed house next to house in random fashion), as well as in their trade, the Cretans had carried into the Early Bronze Age (or Early Minoan period) the traditions developed in Neolithic times. Bronze was introduced, of course, and architecture was becoming more ambitious. The complexity of some of the structures—there was a house at Vasiliki with more than a dozen rooms—is greater than anything yet seen on the mainland of Greece.

The eastern part of Crete was heavily settled during the Early Minoan period, and the people carried on an extensive overseas trade. A hoard of clay sealings at Zygouries has strong affinities with Crete and shows that Minoan traders reached Greece. By the middle of the Early Minoan period the Cretans were making contact with Egypt, and the stone vases found on Crete illustrate the new knowledge which this far-ranging commerce had brought to Crete by 2200 B.C. Business was booming, and the great amount of gold jewelry from the island of Mochlos, off the northeastern coast of Crete, provides a clue to the growing wealth of the civilization. Gold necklaces, bracelets, chains, headbands, and pins with heads carefully worked into patterns of flowers or leaves were buried with the dead. By Early Minoan III, which marked the transition from Early Minoan to Middle Minoan, gold had spread to the center of the island, and north central Crete seems to have made strides into the revolutionary times of the Middle Minoan period, while southern and eastern Crete continued in the earlier traditions.

URBAN REVOLUTION AND THE MIDDLE MINOAN PERIOD. The new developments are indeed startling. The changes began with a radical relocation of the center of civilization on Crete and permeated every aspect of life on the island. The leadership of Minoan civilization shifted to central Crete, and Knossos led the rest of the island to a culture which surpassed in power and elegance anything the Aegean world had seen. Richard Hutchinson, in *Prehistoric Crete,* has called the change an "urban revolution" and all the new developments of this period justify his choice of expression. In 2000 or 1900 B.C., the villages of Crete were suddenly replaced by great cities clustered around palaces and connected by highways. At this time the Minoans began the palace at Knossos. The beginnings were modest, but the plan—blocks of rooms grouped around a central court, with a subsidiary court to the west—set the pattern for later additions. As the building grew, both in the Middle and Late Minoan periods, it maintained a focus on a huge central court.

Developments at Phaestos paralleled those at Knossos. The construction of the palace there was followed by an unprecedented expansion of palace-building at Mallia, northeast of

Knossos, and Gournia, further east. At this time wall paintings began to appear, as well as elaborate water-supply and drainage systems, and the dizzying ascent of Minoan man's capabilities brought him for the first time to the art of writing. Masons' marks and incisions appear on vases, and on seals there are hieroglyphic signs which must have identified the owners. Although some of them resemble Egyptian hieroglyphics in representation of parts of the body or abstract shapes, the language is not Egyptian, and because no connected texts of any length written in these signs have been found, the signs remain indecipherable.

PALACE EXPANSION AND MIDDLE MINOAN CULTURE. In the Middle Minoan II period, great building activity drastically expanded the palaces of Knossos, Phaestos, and Mallia. At Knossos the central court was enlarged, virtually dividing the palace into two great wings. Each wing consisted of dozens of small and large rooms, as well as halls and smaller courts. The palace at this time covered about 100,000 square feet, had a basement and at least some sections more than a single story high. At the same time, methods of writing were improved and a new hieroglyphic system was in wider use on clay bars, labels, and flat tablets, as well as on seals. A numerical system had also been worked out: a vertical stroke for 1, a dot for 10, an oblique stroke for 100, and a lozenge for 1000.

The Minoan civilization had clearly climbed to a high level, sustained by the island's overseas trade. Fragments of Minoan pottery and even complete vases have been found in Egyptian cemeteries, and Egyptian objects have been found on Crete. An Egyptian statue of a man named User was found in the palace of Knossos, and a Babylonian cylinder seal of the reign of Hammurabi (1792-1750 B.C.) found in a Cretan cave. Cretans early in the second millennium B.C. carried on a thriving trade with the eastern part of the Mediterranean, and the wealth that flowed to the island formed the basis for their magnificent creative activity. Island traders crossed the open sea, favored by the etesian winds, and brought their goods to the mouth of the Nile. Then, sailing along the Palestinian coast, past southern Anatolia and the Aegean islands, they returned to Crete with the goods of the East. During this great cultural cross-fertilization, a number of flourishing societies learned from one another. It was also a time of peace. The great palaces were unwalled, and their windows and balconies looked out on the calm green fields of Crete.

EARTHQUAKE AND RECONSTRUCTION. The destruction that razed the palaces did not come at the hands of men. A disastrous earthquake shook the island ca. 1750 B.C. Although the damage was great, the Minoans were resilient; the debris was quickly cleared and rebuilding began. The destruction wrought by the quake not only created the necessity for a new building-period (Middle Minoan III) but, by sealing datable objects in the debris, allows a reasonably accurate estimate of the time at which Middle Minoan II came to an end.

Because it was necessary to rebuild almost from scratch, the palaces took on a new shape. The builders had almost free scope, for they were limited only by the few surviving heavy walls which provided the main lines for the new buildings, as they had for the old. The palace at Knossos, reconstructed at the beginning of Middle Minoan III, lasted for two hundred years. A wide and elaborate staircase with broad shallow steps, flanked by low walls and supported by standing columns, rose two stories to the level of the central court, and then at least one story higher. At this time the Minoan architects introduced another innovation: throughout the palace were left light wells: openings in the ceilings of each room so that the light might filter down from the upper stories to the interior rooms, which otherwise would have been dark and gloomy.

This is also the period of the great wall paintings. At the beginning of Middle Minoan III, or possibly even a little earlier, the great "saffron gatherer" fresco was painted. A magnificent painting of dolphins and flying fish adorned the queen's *megaron,* and elsewhere in the palace there were miniature frescoes of buildings and of groups of people. These paintings are among the most famous of the ancient works of art. When they were discovered at the end of the nineteenth century, the world was stunned by this evidence of so sophisti-

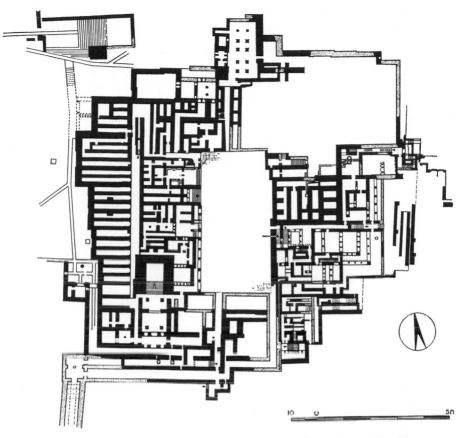

Plan I. The palace at Knossos.

cated an artistic tradition, and it has even been argued that those modern artists who began their own creative lives at that time were influenced by this different style of ancient painting. Certainly the frescoes are a constant reminder of the freshness and grace of the Minoan civilization. The slender, reddish young men, usually bare but for a narrow loincloth, and the women, with their long, many-colored dresses making a bright contrast to their white skin, remain as evidence of a culture which loved beauty and had the wealth to create and enjoy it.

The great practical advance of Middle Minoan III was the

replacement of the old hieroglyphic system with a new, linear script. This script—called Linear A to distinguish it from a later form called Linear B—was inscribed on clay tablets, with a stylus, in lines running from left to right. Although the language of the script has not yet been securely identified, it seems certain that the new script rendered its language syllabically. That is, the language was written in consonant-vowel combinations, with each sign representing the combination of one consonant with one vowel. The new script must have been useful for writing the Cretan language, for the Linear A tablets indicate that much more writing was done in the script than in the hieroglyphic. The tablets all seem to have been commercial accounts: signs, numbers, and totals indicate that the tablets recorded business transactions of some sort. The emergence of the tablets sheds further light on the lives of these early Cretans: they were not only a lively and artistically creative people; they were also a businesslike group who kept records of the more practical aspects of life.

The great foreign trade of the Minoans was seriously affected by a series of international disturbances which struck the Near East at this time. Syria and Mesopotamia were cut off from the West and trade between Egypt and Crete was reduced to a trickle. But the resilient Minoans turned to other markets when the eastern trade decreased, and Minoan imports or influences are found all over the Aegean. At the city of Phylakope, on the island of Melos, frescoes very similar to the Knossos paintings show the influence of Cretan contact; so strong is the similarity that we assume the artists must have either come from Crete or studied there. On the mainland of Greece the fragments of Middle Minoan III pottery found at Mycenae, and the strong Cretan influence on the pottery of Korakou, are evidence of communication with Crete, and a piece of Greek pottery found on Crete indicates that there was trade with the mainland. Undoubtedly the shutting down of trade with the East had turned the attention of the Minoans to the nearer peoples of the north.

Toward the end of the Middle Minoan period, 1600 B.C. or a

little later, another great earthquake damaged the palace of Knossos, but reconstruction proceeded quickly and, at the end of the Middle Minoan period, Minoan civilization was in full vigor. The island entered the Late Minoan period with all the strength and brilliance it had built up over four hundred and fifty years of prosperity.

The Middle Helladic Period:
The Greek Invasion

In Greece itself, however, these years were so different that they were to change the history of the world. The new events began with the great invasions which struck Greece about 2200 B.C. The invaders forced their way through Greece, burning and smashing as they went. The evidence is clear: almost everywhere the ashes of the Early Helladic civilization cover the last level of pottery typical of that culture. After the conflagration came a new world, marked by the almost ubiquitous presence of a totally new kind of pottery. This ware, called Minyan, was a plain, smooth-surfaced pottery made of a high-quality clay which, when baked, took on a color of gray to black, or (in one variety) yellow. Named misleadingly after the legendary Minyan tribes of central Greece, this pottery is the certain identification of the new peoples at a site. Gray Minyan is found in Macedonia, throughout Thessaly, at Eutresis in Boeotia, in great quantities at Korakou near Corinth, at Lerna, at Malthi on the southwest coast of the Peloponnesus, high in the Arcadian mountains at Asea, and at Asine along the northeastern shore of the Gulf of Argos. At almost every site at which the new people left their mark, they left it in the ruins of the earlier settlements. The only important site at which excavation has not revealed evidence of destruction is the rock of Tiryns on the plain of Argos. Unlike its neighbor, Mycenae, which had been razed, Tiryns shows signs of a peaceful transition from Early to Middle Helladic. The Tirynthians, seeing the carnage inflicted by the invaders on nearby Mycenae, may well have decided to let them in peacefully.

37

The invaders settled in most of the towns they had just destroyed. In some cases the remnants of the Early Helladic culture were incorporated into the new communities and, as at Eutresis, a phase immediately after the destruction retains some characteristics of Early Helladic and marks the transition to Middle Helladic. The invaders were clearly less civilized than the peoples they conquered, and they left few memorials apart from the signs of destruction and the Minyan pottery. The level of culture probably dropped when they came into Greece, and the reduced circumstances of most sites at the beginning of the middle Helladic period must be attributed to a less devel-

IX. Grey and yellow Minyan ware.

oped civilization as well as to deliberate destruction. But, once the confusion had subsided, society resumed its progress. The new masters learned from their subjects, and they put to use the technology which had long been developing. Although the tastes and artistic sense of the newcomers had a lasting effect on Helladic society, the techniques and skills of the past lived on adapted to new forms. The layout of the towns remained much as it had been and the methods of manufacture in the ceramics industry were even improved.

The great importance of this invasion for human history lies in the identity of the invaders: they were Greeks. Whatever may be their relationship to the earlier inhabitants, it is known that the language of the Middle Helladic settlers was Greek. From the time they broke into Greece until the end of Mycenaean civilization a thousand years later, the history of Greece is one of unbroken development. There were no later invaders who might have brought the Greek language known to have been spoken by the Mycenaeans. The linguistic and ethnic nature of the Neolithic and Early Helladic people remains a mystery: they may have been of so-called Mediterranean stock, speaking a language as yet unknown; or they may even have been an earlier offshoot of the same group from which the Greek-speaking invaders came. But that the invaders spoke Greek is certain, and henceforth the history of the Aegean is an account of the development of the Hellenic peoples.

LERNA. The excavations of Lerna provide a means of understanding the development of civilization in the Middle Helladic period and, at the same time, neatly demonstrate the distillation of history from the debris of the past. After the destruction of the site marked by the burned remains of the House of the Tiles, houses were much smaller and simpler. Although there is some evidence of earlier traditions in pottery styles, enough changes are apparent to indicate the presence of new people. There is no break between this period and the next, but after a while the Early Helladic elements disappear and Minyan ware and other Middle Helladic pottery types appear and gain predominance. The change in population is confirmed by the change in burial practices: now the remains are found in cist and pit graves within the settlement. Early in this period pottery imports from Crete and the Balkans came to Lerna, and wares were also brought from the island of Aegina and the Cycladic islands. The settlement was thriving and quite large, with many fine houses. The period passed without break into another, represented by two royal graves and also by excellent Middle Helladic pottery.

Thus, the invasions began to strike Greece while the Early Helladic civilization was still in flower, and Lerna was one of the first sites hit. Here, as probably also at Zygouries and perhaps other places, the Greeks forced their way in as early as

2200 B.C. Then they settled down, and for a while their reduced circumstances prevented progress. Contact with Early Helladic peoples, not only at Lerna but at other yet undisturbed centers, preserved a good deal of Early Helladic culture. Invasions were continuing elsewhere, and all Greece was in turmoil. Until the wars were over and destruction ceased, the main impact of the new people was not felt. With peace, and with the rebuilding of settlements all over Greece, the quickening of progress reached Lerna; foreign trade began and rapidly increased. The settlement grew in size and, by the end of the Middle Helladic period, was quite prosperous. The new artistic impulses brought by the Greeks affected pottery styles, and developed and improved until the Late Helladic period, when Lerna— along with the rest of Greece—moved into the brilliance of the Mycenaean epoch. Thus, in the ruins of a single town can be traced the whole arduous development of Greece, from the dark days of invasion to the peak of civilization.

Although some sites, such as Korakou or Eutresis, have few remains of the Middle Helladic settlement, others—like the great city of Malthi in the southwest Peloponnesus—show that the period was a prosperous one. Malthi's walled acropolis was the focus of urban life, and by the end of the Middle Helladic period the central area of the acropolis had been cleared and a palace erected. Farther to the east, the site of Mycenae, which was to become a major center of culture in the Late Helladic period, was growing vigorously.

MYCENAE AND GRAVE CIRCLE B. Until recently, little was known about Mycenae before its period of greatest prosperity. The wealth from the shaft graves which marks the transition to the Late Helladic I period certainly implies the fruition of a long period of growth, but none of the scanty remains of Middle Helladic Mycenae showed how the city had reached the high level to which the gold, silver, and pottery attest. But in 1951 George Mylonas, an American archaeologist who returned to Greece annually to conduct excavations for the Greek Archaeological Society, discovered another grave circle outside the citadel. The discovery of the second group of burials, Grave

Circle B, caused a sensation, for it provided much new information about Middle Helladic Mycenae.

From the graves came handsome vases with geometric spiral designs and stylized pictures of plants. Although the painting was not so elegant as that on Crete in the contemporary Middle Minoan period, the vases from Mycenae were significant artistic creations in their own right. More important, the Middle Helladic pottery from Mycenae showed a natural development from rather simple and uninteresting spiral designs to a rich and imaginative variety, and the vases from the second grave circle were clearly the predecessors of the magnificent ceramics of the Late Helladic period. Mylonas' discovery eliminated doubt that a vital artistic tradition had developed on the Greek mainland in Middle Helladic times. Besides the pottery, an array of precious metal—not so stunning as that discovered by Schliemann but impressive enough—provided evidence of Mycenae's growing wealth. From the first grave came an elaborate gold ornament with embossed circles connected by spiraling lines; another grave yielded a death mask of electrum (an alloy of gold and silver) similar to the death masks found by Schliemann. In still another grave there was a bronze sword sheathed in gold, a vivid memento of some early Greek warrior. Around the bodies in the graves lay gold earrings, and leaf-shaped ornaments of beaten gold. There were gold cups, not so heavily ornamented as later ones, but well made and of similar shape. In one grave, a beautiful duck-shaped rock-crystal bowl lay among crystal-head pins, gold bands, and amber pins, and in almost all the graves there were bronze swords, daggers, knives, and spearheads—reminders, perhaps, of the violence with which the Greeks had come, and the methods by which they had accumulated the wealth they left behind.

THE SPREAD OF TRADE. All this wealth showed that the culture of the invaders had advanced greatly in the centuries after their arrival in Greece. From the handsome but undecorated Minyan pottery and the dull matte-finished pottery had come striking and creative designs in lustrous paint; and out of the destruction that marked the invasion had come unparalleled

X. Middle Helladic vases from Mycenae.

wealth. The source of this renewed prosperity in Greece, as in contemporary Crete, must have been foreign trade. The pottery wares of Asine, on the Gulf of Argos just south of Mycenae, reveal strong influences from the Cycladic islands, and the connections between these islands and Greece brought quantities of Minyan ware to many places in the islands at the beginning of the Middle Cycladic Bronze Age. Similar markings on pottery at Korakou, Lerna, and the Cyclades suggest very close affinities and heavy trade between the Argolid and the islands, and the pieces of Middle Minoan III pottery found at Mycenae suggest a trade with Crete which must have brought financial profit as well as the stimulus of the Minoan artistic tradition.

There is evidence that Greek trade in the Middle Helladic period penetrated far to the west. There are some shards of a peculiar ware in the Aeolian Islands, off the northeastern tip of Sicily, which bear a close resemblance to the Middle Helladic matte-finished ware, and some of which actually are, in all probability, imports of that ware. The existence of a trade route toward the west is supported by the appearance of Minyan pottery in the prehistoric settlement of Ithaca. This evidence indicates that the settlers, as they developed the towns which they inhabited, were exploring and exploiting distant lands to build the prosperity on which their own material progress depended. As the evidence about the Middle Helladic period accumulates, it points strongly to a civilization in Greece, before 1600 B.C., which built vigorous civilized centers on the foundations of an active commerce.

The end of the Middle Helladic period brought almost to its culmination the long climb of Aegean civilization. Through the development of the Neolithic cultures, through the beginnings of prosperous civilization in the Early Helladic period, and through the gradual accretion of wealth, the development of social structure, and the sophistication of artistic endeavor in the Middle Helladic period, the Greek world was being molded and prepared for the civilization of the Mycenaeans.

Often the peoples who had settled in Greece were disrupted; sometimes whole cultures were shattered. The Neolithic civilization, which had itself seen radical change by invasion in Thessaly, changed with the introduction of metal, and the Bronze culture of Early Helladic times was overturned by the Greek invaders who began to break into Greece in. 2200 B.C. Each time a civilization was planted and developed its own resources and creativity, the Aegean world advanced in technology and grew in culture. Each time a new people swept into Greece, the old habits were modified and mingled with those of the newcomers, and new ideas were planted among the old. During the Middle Bronze Age the relationships between the new people on the mainland and the older culture on Crete helped to bring about a kind of cross-fertilization, each group learning from the other—growing in its own way but stimulated by the foreign influences. At the same time, the overseas trade carried on so extensively by the Minoans brought the Aegean world into contact with older and more powerful civilizations in the East and introduced more factors to create change and growth. The changes wrought, the knowledge gained, and the stimuli applied by the invaders to the cultures gave to the Greek world a peculiar homogeneity and creativity. By the end of the Middle Helladic period, the accumulation of artistic knowledge, technical ability, political experience, and commercial wealth was ready to launch the first great civilization on the continent of Europe.

CHAPTER THREE

The Centers of Mycenaean Civilization

The Evidence of Pottery

OF ALL the objects found in the excavations of Mycenaean sites, probably the most useful is the pottery. From ceramics—whether broken and isolated fragments or whole vases—it is possible to build up an entire relative chronology, deducing from the different styles found in successive levels of habitation the developments and changes in the ceramic technique. Once a relative chronology has been established, contemporary levels of different sites can be identified, thus forming a picture of the development of the civilization as a whole. When the relative chronology is fitted into the series of objective dates which even scanty evidence provides, an absolute chronology can be established. The techniques of pottery analysis have evolved from much investigation and testing, and by now the study of ceramics has become almost a subspecialization of archaeology. The learned practitioner can examine a fragment of pottery smaller than a man's hand and—reflecting on the vases he has seen come out of the earth or, perhaps, the pottery he has studied in museums—he can tell the approximate date of its manufacture and the culture to which it belongs; if he knows where it came from, he may be able to use it as evidence for cultural influences.

But before any of these things can be done, the whole ceramic tradition of a civilization must be known and analyzed. Arne Furumark, a Swedish scholar, provided the basic tool for the study of Mycenaean pottery in *The Mycenaean Pottery* and

XI. "Palace Style" vase (LH II).   XII. "Granary Style" vase (LH III).

The Chronology of Mycenaean Pottery (Stockholm, 1941).
Basing his conclusions on the evolution of pottery styles during
the Mycenaean period, Furumark accepted the major division
of pottery into styles belonging to the three Late Helladic periods, and then subdivided these. What he calls Mycenaean I
pottery belongs to the beginning of the Late Helladic period,
and the ceramics of this time show an efflorescence from the
matte-painted pottery styles of the end of the Middle Helladic
period. The spirals and curves running around the vases at the
end of the Middle Helladic period continued into Late Helladic times, and the Minoan influence became stronger in Late
Helladic I. In the pottery of Late Helladic II, zoned decoration gave way to an application of design to the whole surface.
This so-called "palace-style" painting, which appears along
with a more sober decorative technique, produced some of the
most magnificent vases in the history of ceramics. Bold and
colorful stylized birds, plants, and sea creatures painted with
technical perfection on vases a foot or two high attest to the

genius of the Mycenaean artists. At the end of this period floral decoration became more common, leading into the Late Helladic III styles, in which the decorative zone decreases. The designs then appear along the upper parts of the vessels and, later, the whole decoration consists of heavy bands of paint running around the vases. Along with this late "granary-style" painting (named after the granary at Mycenae where many such vessels were found) came a late resurgence of Mycenaean genius in the "close-style" vases. In these, pictorial representation crowds the whole surface in an exciting parallel to the palace-style painting of an earlier time.

With the order of appearance of these styles established, it becomes possible—by noting the changes in the general styles, the shapes of the vessels, and the motifs chosen at different times—to give accurate dates to the styles by means of cross-connections with datable foreign civilizations. Many of the graves in which pieces of Mycenaean pottery have been found also contained objects imported from Egypt and the Near East, and some of the Mycenaean objects themselves show distinct Egyptian influence. These Egyptian connections are extremely valuable, for the long history of writing in Egypt makes an accurate chronology possible there, and precise dates can be given to Egyptian buildings and graves and the objects in them. Thus, when Egyptian objects of known date turn up in Mycenaean graves, the Mycenaean graves and the pottery in them can be assigned corresponding dates. By the same token, when Mycenaean objects are found in Egypt in datable contexts, dates may be determined for them and the knowledge of Mycenaean chronology advances.

The establishment of a chronology is somewhat more complex and sophisticated, but the technique is basically the same. Enough objects can be cross-connected between Egypt and Greece, and between the Mycenaean and other cultures, to give security to the chronology. On this basis, Furumark, splitting the three major divisions of Late Helladic pottery into ten subdivisions, assigned the following absolute dates:

I	1550-1500 B.C.	III B	1300-1230 B.C.
II A	1500-1450	III C:1 (early)	1230-1200
II B	1450-1425	III C:1 (late)	1200-1125
III A:1	1425-1400	III C:2	1125-1100
III A:2 (early)	1400-1375		
III A:2 (late)	1375-1300		

This chronology is not accepted by all students of Mycenaean civilization. Some scholars argue for revisions of specific dates; others doubt the feasibility of dating styles within twenty-five year periods and the wisdom of establishing such minute subdivisions. But the Furumark scheme deserves to stand, even if only partially correct, because it is the logical working out of an analysis the basic methods of which are not questioned. The scheme itself is certainly close enough to fact that its general outline provides a satisfactory chronological basis for determining the dates of the events which overtook the Mycenaeans. When a specific date is given to the construction or destruction of a building, it is based on this scheme or one very much like it: that is, the date is dictated by the pottery found in the ruins —the earliest pottery establishes the date of construction, and the latest pottery indicates when the building fell out of use or was destroyed. For archaeologist and historian alike, the pottery is an indispensable tool for establishing the sequence of events and providing a chronology for the Mycenaean civilization.

Besides providing a basis for chronology, the study of pottery can demonstrate the wide-ranging and generally unified culture which the Mycenaeans created in Greece. These styles of pottery make their appearance not only at Mycenae, but at Pylos, Thebes, Korakou, and Zygouries. All over the Greek mainland —in graves and scattered on the surface of the earth—broken fragments of pottery lie as reminders of Mycenaean habitation and proof of the unity of that civilization. The vases and shards, sharing the characteristics of painting styles and motifs, are persuasive evidence of the close connections between all the Mycenaean towns, and the pottery is so widespread that we can only conclude that the great civilization of Greece, at the end of the second millennium B.C., was the common culture of the Greeks.

The Palace of Mycenae

Although the pottery of these long-vanished people is of supreme importance to an understanding of what they built, it is not pottery which has attracted modern man's attention to the Mycenaean civilization. The massive remains of the buildings and walls have stood for centuries as enigmatic monuments to an ancient world. Pausanias was struck by these reminders of the past: he noted (in II, XVI, 5) that "parts of the wall are left, and the gate, on which lions stand. These too are said to be the works of the Cyclopes, who built the wall at Tiryns." Pausanias knew also of the tombs at Mycenae (which, he thought, contained the bones of some of the famed heroes of the *Iliad* and of Greek tragedy) and wrote of the treasures buried there. Pausanias' account, forgotten or derided for centuries, has now proved basically correct. There are tombs at Mycenae, there was a treasure beneath the earth, and the walls once encompassed a city built long before the birth of the cities we call Hellenic. But what Pausanias saw was only a fraction of the original city—only a very small part of what today, almost two thousand years after his time, has been opened to the eyes of men by a half-century's labor. For the first time since the destruction of the city more than three thousand years ago, men can look upon the magnificent works of these ancient architects.

The great pork-chop-shaped wall runs the entire circuit of the hilltop, surrounding the citadel and pierced at the northwest by the great gate over which are poised the two carved lions that guard the road. The path inside the gate leads past a large grain warehouse on the right, up a broad ramp which runs by Schliemann's treasure-filled grave circle and a group of houses, and finally up into the main citadel area. Directly

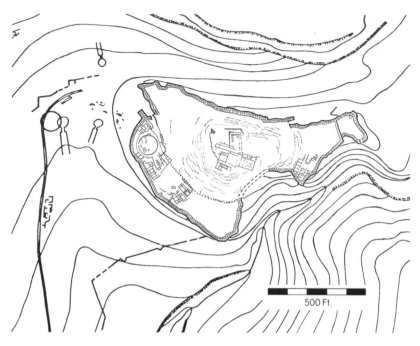

Plan II. The palace at Mycenae.

ahead, one hundred feet off, lie the ruins of a large house; to the left, three hundred or more yards away, is the far wall of the citadel; only sixty yards ahead lies the great palace.

The palace area was the whole walled citadel before the Late Helladic period. By Late Helladic I the palace, adapted to the terrain, stood in the center of an enlarged citadel, and by 1400 B.C. (that is, Late Helladic III) this older palace was gone and a new one stood in its place. Perhaps the earlier building was destroyed by fire; there is some evidence to support such a conclusion. Whatever the reason, a new palace was created in Late Helladic III and it is this building, though severely damaged by time, which stands today. What remains comprised mainly the public rooms, for many of the subsidiary rooms were destroyed in an early excavation which was carelessly carried down to the original rock of the hill. The public rooms lie along the east-west axis of the palace, facing the plain of Argos to the south. A grand stairway sweeps up fifteen feet to an ante-room which opens into the throne room. The visitor then crosses a great court to the east, steps between two columns and across a porch, and passes through another anteroom into a great *megaron* about fifty feet long and thirty-five feet wide. The stuccoed floor of this fine room, resurfaced four times, shows long use and careful maintenance. In the center of the floor stood a raised circular hearth about ten feet in diameter, set off by four wooden columns. With frescoes adorning walls and reflecting the blaze in the great hearth, with the sunlight streaming in from the doors and perhaps from windows as well, and with men in armor standing near their painted replicas on the walls, the *megaron* in its prime must have been a truly royal chamber.

The whole complex of public rooms was laid out with care

XIII. Rooms of the palace at Mycenae.

and deliberation. The plan, unlike that of the earlier palace, made no concession to the dictates of terrain. When these rooms were added to the older part of the palace, new walls abutting old were thickened at one end so that the new wing would lie at an axis slightly different from that of the rest of the palace, and the terrain on which the rooms were to stand was modified to permit the builder to execute his conception. Any parts of the building which remained were boldly leveled, and some of the ground itself was cut away to provide a level base. At the eastern end of the wing a great amount of fill was poured in (the perimeter fortification wall acted as a retainer) and the base was thus extended to make room for all the floor space the architect needed. These important rooms stretched along the heights facing the south, and the whole contour of the site was drastically altered to suit the plan.

The Mycenaean builder's skills and his mastery of engineering appear again and again in the structures which still stand. When the architects turned to the construction of tombs, they showed their genius in the creation of structures as brilliant as they are different from palaces. The *tholos* tomb, a large round chamber with a domed roof, is almost a hallmark of Mycenaean civilization. The so-called Treasury of Atreus, an underground tomb outside the citadel of Mycenae and below the lower town, exemplifies the Mycenaean mastery of complex problems in structural engineering. A cement-paved approach, flanked by walls lined with huge well-cut blocks of stones, runs directly into the tomb. A door, capped by an enormous lintel weighing over a hundred tons, opens into the depths of the hill. Above the door, shadowed in black, an open triangular arch relieves the weight of stone pressing down upon it. A short corridor leads to the main chamber, a circular room almost fifty feet in diameter. Its walls, successive courses of smoothly cut stone, rise almost forty-five feet, curving with mathematical exactness to finish in a perfect dome.

This masterpiece of precision, built about 1330 B.C., reveals perhaps more clearly than any other single structure the technical accomplishment of the Mycenaean builder. He was no mere

XIV. Approach to the "Treasury of Atreus."

piler of stones, but an engineer and architect in every sense of the terms. His control of weight and stress in the construction of the great dome shows a technical mastery which would have done credit even to the Romans. Nor was this tomb an accidental flash of genius. Although it is the largest tomb of its type, other *tholos* tombs dot the mainland of Greece. The Mycenaeans were capable of reproducing this complex structure again and again, and it might well be supposed that Mycenaean architects were specialists whose professional lives were devoted to building and to training technicians for the future.

The Palace at Pylos

The architectural tradition found at Mycenae also flourished elsewhere in Greece. The recent excavations at Pylos in the southwestern Peloponnesus have opened to view a Mycenean palace the whole floor plan of which is almost entirely preserved. As at Mycenae, this palace surmounts a hill astride an

53

important road—the north-south route along the western shore of the Peloponnesus. As at Mycenae, the terrain was altered to accommodate the architect's plan. The remains of walls around the palace area show that earlier buildings had been pulled down to make room for new construction, and the contour of the land beneath the new foundations indicates that the whole top of the ridge had been cut down and leveled as a preliminary to building.

The palace stretches across the top of the hill in three wings, all dating to the middle of Late Helladic III—about 1300 B.C. or a little after (the westernmost wing was probably built just a little earlier than the other two). As at Mycenae, a part of the palace is given over to public rooms; at Pylos, the central part serves this purpose.

A single column provides a focus at the center of the portico;

XV. Interior of the "Treasury of Atreus."

at the left (still outside the entrance to the palace) a door leads into two rooms of great importance to the commercial business of the king and of supreme value to our knowledge of the Mycenaean world. These are the famous Pylos archive rooms, the part of the palace to which incredible good fortune guided Blegen's first trial trench in 1939. Out of this trench came the hundreds of clay tablets which proved that the mainlanders were literate—the tablets which, together with the fruits of later excavation, were to prove that the language of Linear B was Greek. In these rooms were kept the records of tax payments and other contributions to the kings who occupied the palace. And although tablets were found scattered in other parts of the palace, it is quite clear that these archive rooms were the main repository. Here sat the scribes, on the low bench which runs around three walls of the interior room. Here the scribes fashioned the clay, patting and smoothing it into even-surfaced tablets ready for writing. Here they inscribed the needed information, stacking the finished tablets on wooden shelves placed against the walls. Here, still outside the entrance, easily accessible to visitors, the royal officials tallied the arrivals and departures of people and goods.

Another single column inside the door marks the entrance to a large court open to the sky. To the left, among a group of rooms, a benched waiting room offers hospitality to guests. Directly across from the portico, two more columns flank the entrance to the state rooms. The visitor walks between these through a vestibule with brightly painted floor and walls and into the great throne room, which is forty-two feet long and thirty-seven feet wide. As in the *megaron* of Mycenae, the center of the hall was occupied by a circular raised hearth flanked by four columns. Here again the brilliance of the Mycenaean artists left its light on the painted walls. A pair of griffins look out from the frescoes behind the throne. Elsewhere a man playing a lyre is shown. The floor was painted in a series of squares, each with a different multicolored linear pattern. The square directly before the throne bears a representation of a giant octopus. Above all this elegance was a balcony, along the walls, supported by the four central columns. Directly above the hearth in the middle of the room, an opening in the ceiling let in light and air and allowed the smoke to pass out through a clay chimney-pipe which ran up through the roof.

In this spacious chamber the kings of Pylos conducted state business, met ambassadors, received petitions, and rendered judgments. The throne room itself is surrounded on three sides by storage chambers, reached by two long corridors running along two sides of the throne room. The corridors can be entered either from the great open court or through doors in the side of the vestibule. Just across from the vestibule doors, stairways lead to the upper floor of the building. One of the storage rooms on the left, or western, corridor contained 2853 *kylixes*—tall, champagne-glass-shaped drinking cups made of pottery—all found crushed into thousands of small pieces by the destruction which struck the palace. In a long double chamber directly behind the throne room, the palace store of olive oil was kept in great jars sunk deep into raised stands.

Toward the front of the palace, at the right of the great court, another passageway leads into an external court which, paved with stucco and with water piped in, probably served as a private retreat. Nearby another room emphasizes the private aspect of this part of the palace and suggests the atmosphere of seclusion which it must have provided. Here stands an ancient bathtub, still intact, as it was used by the kings of Pylos over three thousand years ago. This terracotta tub, shaped rather like a violin, was set into a clay base against the southeastern wall of the room. In front of it, a step permits easy access to the bath. Against the wall near the tub were found two great water jars four feet high; at the bottom of the big jugs lay small vessels for dipping.

On the other side of the wall against which the tub was placed, but reached through a corridor which led from a two-columned portico off the open court, there is a smaller throne room, probably reserved for the queen's use. Although it does not have the central columns of the large *megaron,* the room did have a hearth in the middle, and its frescoed walls carried

XVI. Reconstruction of the palace at Pylos.

Plan III. The palace complex at Pylos.

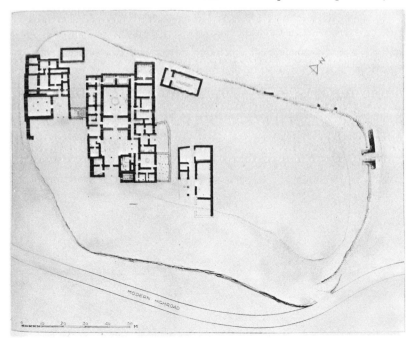

XVII. The bathtub at Pylos.

life-sized pictures of lions, leopards, and other animals. The eastern wall of the room opens onto an open court (similar to the king's court), at the southern end of which a corridor leads separately into two small rooms. These two rooms actually face the front of the palace, but there is no access to them except through the corridor from the interior open court. One of these rooms, which had an underground drain, clearly was a bathroom or lavatory; the other, reached through a small corridor which separated it from the first, had elegantly painted walls, floor, and (probably) ceiling. The floor was divided into forty-nine squares, with the perimeter row given over to more abstract linear patterns, and the inner squares to dolphins, octopi, and fishes. The little corridor between the two rooms had a beautifully decorated floor composed of three rows of seven squares. The side rows were painted with abstract designs; the middle row, with realistic pictures—one of which, an octopus, remains almost intact, while traces of a group of three dolphins are still to be found in the second square.

The interpretation of this group of rooms as the queen's wing is almost surely correct. It has a room of state—the *megaron* with hearth—and its own sanitary facilities. The elegance of the corridor and one of the two rooms off it seems to give that area the touch of a boudoir, and the location of the whole complex—in an outside corner of the palace—must have given the rooms a bright and airy atmosphere. The rooms, entered only from the interior of the palace, were somewhat protected, but they were not really any more isolated or difficult of access than any other group of private rooms. The architectural plan for women fits the picture of their rather free and open life gained from paintings found on the walls of this and other palaces.

All these rooms—central court, archive area, state chambers, storerooms, and queen's quarters—comprise the central block of the palace. Here the royal family lived; here the main business of the kingdom was conducted; here the political life of the whole southwestern Peloponnesus was focused. But there was more to the palace, and its plan and use cannot be completely understood unless its other parts are examined.

Northeast of the main block lies a rectangular wing consisting of three large workrooms. In the middle of the open southwestern corner stands a limestone block coated with plas-

XVIII. Reconstruction of part of the painted floor in the queen's apartment.

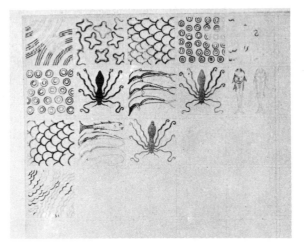

59

ter and with traces of painted decoration. An altar probably once stood there, and a small room facing it on the south may have served as a shrine. One of the tablets found here names a goddess, Potnia Hippeia, indicating that this was probably the area in which the religious life of the palace was conducted. To the north of this building, the end of an aqueduct reveals the source of the palace's water: a pipe brought it in from the northeast, branching off to take the water into the king's court, among other places. Off at a distance, to the north of the aqueduct, a free-standing building stored the palace's wine in huge jars sunk into the ground, ending the palace complex in this area.

There is a whole separate building on the other side of the palace, toward the west. Built a little earlier than the rest, it was once an independent palace with its own courts, halls, and throne room. When the new central palace rose, it was perhaps turned over to another member of the royal family who needed the state rooms and could put to good use the still elegant though smaller palace. Stone column bases mark the entrance to a reception hall, the walls of which are decorated with a row of pink griffins. In the center of the hall stood a single column; aligned with it, in the middle of the hall's left wall, there was a door leading into the main state room. So much of the floor has been carried away over the years that it is difficult to visualize the layout of the room. That four columns were set in a square near the door is certain, and there may have been two other columns at the other end of the room to make two rows of three columns each. There may also have been a hearth, either in the center of the four columns or elsewhere, but not a trace of it is left, and the arrangement of the hall—with a turn into the three rooms—was that used for Mycenaean rooms of state before the straight-line arrangement of the main palace was devised.

To the northwest of the great hall a complex of large and small rooms provided at least part of the living quarters for the older palace, and a room with a drain cut through the outside northwestern wall shows that the royal quarters had plumbing even before the newer palace was built. A separate building to the north of this complex, with a number of jar bottoms still sunk in the earth, shows that this older palace also had a separate wine magazine for the storage of the great quantities of wine kept in readiness for palace functions.

The whole palace of Pylos covers about an acre and a half of the top of the hill; thus, although not an enormous building, it was sizable, complex, and elegant. The part that remains today was occupied from about 1300 B.C. to about 1230 B.C., and it is the most complete example of Mycenaean architecture at the time when the civilization was at its peak. The architects were able to control the terrain to create buildings which were well

XIX. Gallery at Tiryns.

organized and carefully thought out. The buildings featured many practical advantages: running water, interior plumbing, and roomy quarters. The whole architectural tradition reflects a culture of great artistic talent. Profusely decorated with ingenious and brilliantly inspired paintings executed with a technical proficiency of which any graphic tradition could be proud, the buildings surrounded their inhabitants with an atmosphere of great beauty. Under its roof all kinds of activity went on: potters made and painted crockery; metal-workers hammered and cast bronze; the scribes recorded the business affairs of the king; servants or slaves scurried to and fro, carrying wine and oil; ambassadors and lords met with the king or other officials in the rooms of state. The palace served as the center for all the political and economic life of a busy kingdom, and was itself—in all its splendor and beauty—a symbol of the talent of the Mycenaeans and the wealth of their kings.

Tiryns, Gla, and Others

There are other Mycenaean palaces at important sites in Greece, and they all are basically the same as the structures at Mycenae and Pylos. One of these, known even in antiquity, is that at Tiryns, situated on a rock rising abruptly out of the plain of Argos about a mile from the sea. A massive fortification surrounds the flat area on the top of the rock; the wall, thirty to fifty feet thick, is pierced by lateral galleries which permitted the defenders to move about in safety. The palace has some resemblance to that of Mycenae, though its shape is limited by the actual space available within the walls. A vestibule and portico lead to the throne room, which has a hearth surrounded by four columns, just as at Mycenae and Pylos. The open courts and subsidiary rooms are also typical of Mycenaean architecture. The positions of the main entrance (to the left of the central court) and the state rooms (which face the middle of the court across from the entrance) are identical with the arrangement at Pylos. The walls of this palace, like those of Mycenae and Pylos, were adorned with brilliant paintings, and

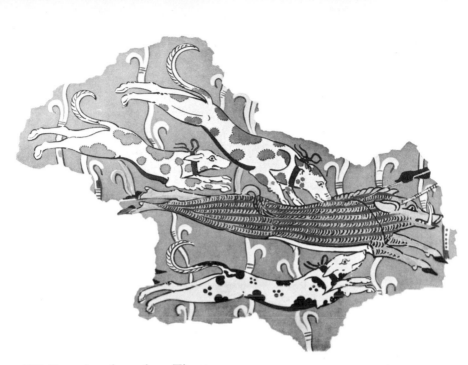

XX. Boar chase fresco from Tiryns.

here were found some of the most beautiful and famous of all the Mycenaean frescoes. Dogs chase and worry a wounded boar; deer stand gracefully near each other or leap about; warriors march along in a line; a chariot rolls slowly past stylized trees. All these scenes and more decorated the walls. The square subdivisions of the floors, painted with figures of dolphins and octopi, show virtual identity with those of Pylos. All in all, the palace at Tiryns, built during Late Helladic III and occupied from about 1425 B.C. to 1100 B.C., shows close affinities with the buildings at Mycenae and Pylos.

Mycenaean palace-building was not limited to the Peloponnesus. There was a palace at Thebes in Boeotia, and another nearby at Gla on an island in the middle of Lake Kopais. This island, uncannily similar in shape to the acropolis at Mycenae, is about 3000 feet long, more than double the size of the citadel at Mycenae, and was completely encircled by a wall like that of

Tiryns. It is a great pity that this site, examined so little and so long ago, has only recently begun to receive the attention of modern archaeologists. Even so, enough was turned up in 1893 to indicate that this was the center of another Mycenaean power. The circuit wall alone surpasses any fortification yet known. What was called the palace—an L-shaped structure with one wing running along the northern wall of the fort, the other extending into the interior, and with corridors running along the interior of the L to connect over a dozen rooms of good size—shows all the characteristics of good Mycenaean construction. Besides this palace on Goulas Island, the excavation recently begun at Iolkoᶜ, at the northern end of the Gulf of Volo, shows that there too, at the traditional capital of the kings of Thessaly, a Mycenaean palace once stood.

XXI. The palace at Gla.

Art and Artifacts

Much about the life of the Mycenaeans can be read from the ruins of these palaces. Their mere existence in so many places shows that Mycenaean political power was concentrated at a number of sites. The construction of all these buildings began fairly early in the Late Helladic period, and this indicates that the development of power and the accumulation of wealth to which the palaces attest originated in the Middle Helladic period. In that earlier time, which saw no mean accomplishments, the Mycenaeans were still consolidating their position in Greece and expanding their foreign trade, but they had not yet turned their attention to large-scale construction. Within the palaces themselves the remains of frescoes, beautiful as they may be, are mere hints of the great sophistication of representational art in the Late Helladic period, and the thousands upon thousands of clay vessels found at Pylos only suggest the extent of the royal wealth and palace facilities. The extraordinary virtuosity of the architects, who controlled the terrain and mastered the principles of engineering to put up complex and extensive buildings, is a tribute to the technical abilities of the Mycenaeans. The similarities in the plans of the different palaces indicate that the science of architecture had benefited from wide-ranging exchanges of ideas and information.

The wealth which the Mycenaean palaces suggest the living enjoyed is confirmed by finds in the houses of the dead. The knowledge of the riches of this society, first revealed by Schliemann's startling discoveries, has been a motivating force behind the study of Mycenae. Schliemann produced one of the greatest and most astounding treasures ever found by archaeologists, and Mylonas' discovery of the second grave circle extended our knowledge of the development of the Mycenaean economy. Gold jewelry and sword hilts found in the graves show that Mycenae was wealthy by the end of the Middle Helladic period. The deposits in the Late Helladic shaft graves of Grave Circle A, Schliemann's discovery, were incomparably

XXII. Part of the treasure from Mycenae, Grave Circle A (in the National Museum, Athens).

richer. Out of Graves IV and V, dated soon after the beginning of Late Helladic I (about 1550 B.C.), came extraordinarily well-worked gold cups, a silver bowl with little inlaid gold heads, and a tall gold goblet with two handles topped by doves nibbling daintily at the rim. There were bronze daggers inlaid with gold and silver scenes of hunting and animal life, animal-shaped drinking vessels, a lion's head in gold leaf, and a silver bull's head with horns and mouth of gold. The faces of the corpses were covered with hammered gold death masks, and five of these ancient portraits were found. Around the female skulls lay golden diadems and headbands. In Grave III, slightly later in date than Graves IV and V, lie the bodies of two children, completely wrapped in gold foil; the clothing of the women in this grave was decorated with more than 700 small discs with repoussé designs on their faces. A catalog of all the items of precious metal found would fill pages.

There can be no doubt of Mycenae's wealth in the sixteenth century B.C. Unfortunately, few kings except those of Mycenae had the good fortune to lie in their tombs undisturbed, and there is little elsewhere to compare with the Mycenaean treas-

XXIII. Inlaid dagger from Mycenae.

ure. Over the centuries, treasure-seekers, curious tourists, and antiquarians have systematically plundered the tombs. Most of the surreptitious digging was conducted by ordinary thieves, and there is no doubt that hundreds of Mycenaean cups and ornaments have been melted and remade into modern jewelry, coins, and even fillings for teeth. Yet enough remains at other places in Greece to give some indication that the elegant accoutrements in the graves at Mycenae, rare as they are today, were once buried with the royal dead in countless graves all over the Greek mainland. For example, out of a *tholos* tomb at a little town named Vaphio, in the central Peloponnesus, came two cups of gold wrought in the most marvelous fashion, with scenes of men wrestling bulls and tying them. The burial, dated by pottery to between 1550 B.C. and 1425 B.C., is an indication of the richness of the Mycenaean tombs. Across the Peloponnesus at Pylos no unplundered tombs have yet been found, but in the litter of one lay a gold royal seal along with two gold rings and some ornaments; in another, some gold beads and pieces of ivory which had been overlooked indicated that the burial offering had once been rich. Within the palace itself a little gold head, like those which adorned the silver bowl from

Mycenae, lay in the dirt—a sad reminder of these gorgeous vessels once carried about the palace for use at royal feasts.

There is more evidence of wealth in the expensive grave offerings from a tomb at Dendra, southeast of Mycenae on the Argive plain. This later *tholos* tomb seems to belong to the middle of the fourteenth century B.C. and is evidence of the continued prosperity of the Mycenaean civilization. Here were gold and silver cups, gold jewelry and gold leaf, ivories, swords with gold hilts—all the accoutrements of the earlier graves at Mycenae. Among a neighboring group of chamber tombs, the second, containing some gold objects and a silver cup, is no earlier than 1200 B.C. Nearby at Prosymna, just north of the city of Argos, a number of Late Helladic II and III tombs yielded gold jewelry and ornaments, while from Late Helladic I tombs came handsome daggers of bronze inlaid with gold and silver and fitted with hilts of gold. The dates of these finds confirm the evidence from Mycenae that the civilization reached great heights as early as 1550 B.C., and the concord between the precious objects at Prosymna and Dendra shows that this material wealth lasted well into the late Helladic period.

Outside the Peloponnesus, gold objects were found in Late Helladic tombs at Athens and Thorikos in Attica. Farther to the north, gold ornaments came from a Late Helladic III tomb

XXIV. Bowl with inlaid heads from Mycenae.

XXV. Gold jewelry
from Dendra.

near Pteleos in Thessaly. Citation after citation could be made
of tombs throughout Greece which, though plundered in antiquity and in modern times, still contain a few tiny pieces of gold
or silver. These bits of precious metal, cast aside in the
scramble for heavier loot, were found lying in the debris as
reminders of the long-gone wealth and glory of the men whose
bones lie in the dust.

All this precious metal must have come from the prosperity
which vigorous commerce had created for the Mycenaeans. No
area in Greece had a monopoly on wealth, and all the Mycenaean cities participated in the commerce as it expanded
during the Middle Helladic period. The accumulation of
wealth had reached great heights everywhere by Late Helladic
I, or 1550 B.C., and the economic prosperity of the Mycenaeans
lasted well into Late Helladic III. All the evidence of pottery,
architecture, and painting, along with the marvelous grave
offerings, yield a coherent and consistent picture of the nature
of Mycenaean society. All the arts were pursued with vigor and
received the benefits of a highly developed technical tradition.
The engineering which produced the great edifices bespeaks a
mechanical and even mathematical knowledge of high order,
and the ceramic and metal objects were created by craftsmen

whose abilities have never been surpassed. All this suggests a culture of diversity and specialization with trained artisans pursuing their own trades and working precious materials into magnificent pieces of art.

Each Mycenaean center benefited from the great artistic tradition, and each center boasted a great palace. The towns surrounded the palaces, and the prosperity of the society as a whole was turned to the well-being of the rulers, creating luxury for their lives and glory for their deaths. Each town seems to have been royally oriented, each king gathering to himself the most talented men to create a palace that would stand as a monumental demonstration of his power. And yet, although there were many individual centers of power, the culture was

XXVI. Terracotta head from Mycenae.

remarkably unified. Ceramic styles and techniques were strikingly similar all over Greece, and the plans of palaces and designs of tombs were basically the same from one place to another. Artists probably traveled from city to city to execute commissions, and young men must have been free to take apprenticeships in the shops of the great. Many Mycenaeans must have traveled about to work and trade, for the community of taste on which a unified style rests could have resulted only from a great deal of communication. The homogeneity of this culture suggests trading caravans rather than armies, friendly visits rather than hostile attacks—a period of peace in which busy people carried on all kinds of private and public business without fear. The people of Mycenaean Greece, although situated in towns and cities far apart, must have felt bound to each other by similar customs and practices. This combination of material prosperity and homogeneity of civilization has rarely been equalled.

CHAPTER FOUR

Records of the Past

EVER SINCE THE MYCENAEAN CIVILIZATION WAS REDISCOVERED, the ethnic origin of the people and their language has been disputed. Some scholars maintained that the "Achaeans," as these people were called, were part of a Mediterranean group—culturally, linguistically, and ethnically different from Indo-European peoples—that settled in the Mediterranean area about 1000 B.C. Other scholars argued that the Mycenaeans were actually Greeks who came into the Greek peninsula about 2000 B.C. These scholars based their argument on the following evidence: after the fall of the Mycenaean civilization, a gradual change from Mycenaean pottery styles to Greek geometric styles can be observed at certain sites. Because there was no sudden disruption after Mycenaean times, and because the makers of the geometric pottery were Greek, so also must the Mycenaeans have been Greek. And because there had been no cultural break between the beginning of the Middle Helladic period and Mycenaean times, these Greeks must have arrived at the time of the great destructions of 2100-1900 B.C.

This argument, although reasonable, did not convince everyone; nevertheless, it steadily gained ground in the years before and immediately after World War II. Then, the decipherment of one of the linear scripts settled the language problem.

The Decipherment of Linear B

Ever since Sir Arthur Evans' excavations at Knossos the world had known that the Minoan culture was literate. Evans found three kinds of writing on Crete: a hieroglyphic script, an early linear script (Linear A), and a later linear script (Linear B). Because all the tablets with writing were found on Crete, Evans and most others believed that the language itself was Minoan—whatever that was—and that the mainlanders had been illiterate. But when Blegen turned up more than six hundred tablets at Pylos in 1939, the old theories were turned upside down. Almost everyone conceded that the civilization in Greece, as well as that on Crete, had been literate. As more and more tablets came out of the ground when Blegen resumed his digging after the war, a young British architect, Michael Ventris, began to work on their decipherment.

A number of major advances in the late 1940s and early 1950s had armed Ventris with new tools. Alice Kober, by showing alternations in the syllabic endings of words, had demonstrated that Linear B represented an inflected language. New excavations produced more tablets. In 1951 Emmett L. Bennett, Jr., codified the texts and published the material inscribed on the tablets found in 1939. Ventris analyzed the signs and built up what information he could about them, circulating the results of his study—to scholars interested in the problem—in some twenty mimeographed "Work Notes." He aligned the signs on a complex grid, allotting to each column of the grid those signs which seemed to have vowels in common. By February 1952 Ventris had placed the majority of the signs in a theoretical relationship to one another. As he worked, he speculated about the identity of the language, at length coming to believe that it was Etruscan, the still mysterious language of the early inhabitants of northern Italy. But even with this belief, he tested in Note 20 a number of tentative identifications, such as *ko-wo* and *ko-wa,* which could be interpreted in Greek to mean *boy* and *girl,* and *to-so* and *to-sa,* inflected variants of the Greek *so many.* Nevertheless, Ventris ended the note without accepting the identifications. Yet while his latest work was still in the mail to his colleagues, the full impact of his suggestions struck him. He could not escape the conclusion that the language was Greek. Applying the identifications of the signs to other tablets, new words jumped forth: *smith, potter, priest,*

73

XXVII. First linear B tablet found on the Greek mainland.

and *priestess;* the declension of nouns was that of early Greek. As he applied the identified signs to words with signs still unknown, the decipherment broadened to include more words and yield values for more signs. Ventris had accomplished one of the great scholarly feats of all time: he had broken through the barriers which obscured the earliest texts written in an Indo-European language. Linear B was Greek.

Ventris was now joined by a young English philologist, John Chadwick. The fruits of their joint effort were published in 1953. Their theory was beginning to win adherents when a new discovery at Pylos virtually confirmed it. Blegen wrote to Ventris that the decipherment of a newly unearthed tablet had produced the word *ti-ri-po,* the Greek *three-legged pot,* and an ideogram portraying just such a vessel supported the transcription;

other transcribed words were also supported by ideograms. With this confirmation of the decipherment, most scholars abandoned their arguments and hailed the achievement.

Now the skills of all the disciplines used in the study of antiquity were turned to the examination of the texts of these tablets. Historians accepted the identification of the Greek language as the last piece of evidence required to prove that these early inhabitants of Greece were the ancestors of the classical Greeks. Philologists and linguists whose hypotheses about the earlier state of the Greek language were confirmed felt the rare excitement of men whose conjectures have been proven right. The texts of the tablets offered a wealth of material to be mined for evidence about the structure of Mycenaean society, and the new tablets coming each year from the excavations at Pylos and Mycenae provided an ever-increasing body of material for study.

The Nature of the Tablets

The texts themselves are only records and, in general, records only of the most mundane and everyday activities. But 'from these "laundry lists," as the tablets might be called derisively, painstaking work has culled a great deal of information. The Pylos group, a hoard of palace accounts written just before the destruction, has made possible the most exciting insights. The unbaked clay tablets, carefully stored on shelves in the archive room of the palace, were baked hard by the conflagration that extinguished Mycenaean civilization in the western Peloponnesus. Like the legendary phoenix which arises from its own ashes, the tablets came forth from the flames to bring the Mycenaean society back to life.

The tablets contain inventories of goods, and a careful balancing of some of the accounts shows almost the full amount of the record of certain categories. It is also clear that the tablets baked in the fire were, so to speak, current accounts, but it is difficult to be sure about the length of the accounting period. Some entries dealing with land are in duplicate; accounts on a number of small tablets are repeated and collated on a few larger ones. It seems that the scribes carefully recorded information on the smaller tablets and then, when all the accounts were in, they assembled the multitude of texts on the more convenient larger tablets. This procedure suggests that the period in which the tablets were prepared must have been long enough to allow the accumulation of enough smaller tablets to justify the transfer of information to the larger ones. Yet even this indication of bureaucratic activity need not be taken to indicate a period of more than a few weeks. The details of those records that remain show a system elaborate enough to produce thousands of such tablets over any longer span of time. Unfortunately, it will probably never be known for certain just how long the accounting period actually was, but it seems likely that the accounts cover transactions over a rather short time.

Pylian Geography

Enough information was assembled, however, to provide many valuable clues to the organization of the Pylian kingdom. Geographic and administrative information can be distilled from an analysis of the many place names on the tablets. All together, over two hundred locations are named on the tablets, but this need not mean that there were two hundred separate towns. Some of the names may refer only to tiny hamlets, or possibly to streets in larger towns. Even so, the large number of place names indicates a fairly complex geography. All these names, even the hundred or so which appear only once in the tablets, must have had some administrative meaning. The Ptolemaic bureaucracy in Egypt, where city streets had officials responsible to higher officials, makes it clear that ancient red tape was as tangled as its modern version. Thus it is more than likely that every place mentioned in the Pylos tablets had some individual identity in the administration of the Pylian territory.

Some of the places were obviously larger and more important than others. The area subject to Pylos was divided into two administrative districts: *De-we-re A-ko-ra-i-io* (the "Hither District"), and *Pe-ra A-ko-ra-i-io* (the "Farther District"). The scribes' careful records have left some clues about these districts, and their consistent grouping of a series of nine towns on a number of tablets permits identification of the major towns in the Hither District. These nine towns were among the most important, and a study of their assessments or contributions shows them in the top 10 per cent of all the cities in the province. On one tablet the group of nine is followed by a group of seven more, and these seem to have been the major centers of the Farther District. Statistically, this group has smaller quantities attributed to it than the group of nine, but it comes ahead of most of the rest of the names. Although none of these towns can yet be located geographically, the accounting methods reveal that the palace had a highly organized concept of the arrangement of the provinces, and perhaps in these lists indicated the chief towns of the provincial subdivisions.

There is no doubt that the whole structure of assessment was carefully thought out. Many of the towns that dealt in only one kind of product lead almost all others in the assessment of that particular commodity, and it seems that the organized assessment made certain towns specialists in livestock, grain, or some other suitable product. The list of officials shows that each town had its *Ko-re-te*, who was responsible for the assessment; the bureaucracy even extended to a *Po-ro-ko-re-te*, who was a deputy to the village official. All these were supervised by the central bureaucracy at the palace. In fact, a record of an inspection trip made to some of the outlying towns was left among the tablets to show Pylos' attention to the affairs of the distant towns.

Thus, from the tablets, some concept of the administrative arrangement of the western Peloponnesus begins to emerge. A large palace contained the records of commodities from distant areas. Throughout the land subject to the "Wanax," or king, minor officials scurried to meet their quotas, sending their assessments to Pylos, and quaking as the royal inspectors made

MYCENAEAN SITES IN
SOUTHWEST PELOPONNESUS

MAP III

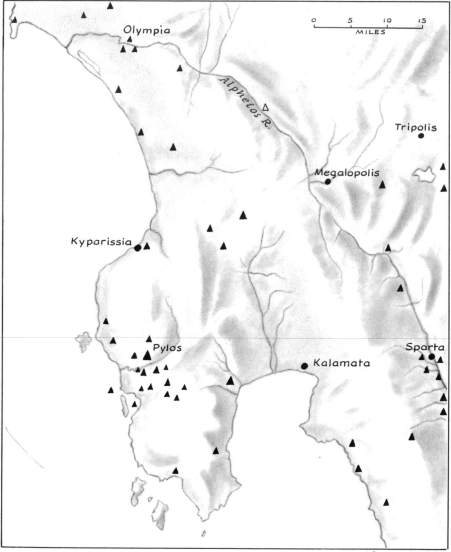

After McDonald.

their rounds from town to town. Perhaps, as excavation proceeds, archaeologists will some day bring from the earth the ruins of these ancient towns which today live only in name.

Property and Real Estate

The tablets are also useful in providing a picture of the political arrangement of the Pylian kingdom, but they are even more significant for the study of the objects of finery and furniture destroyed in the last fire. Besides the cloaks and cloths, mixing bowls, baskets, vases, and cups listed in the accounts, the minutely detailed records provide an extensive picture of the furniture. One tablet tells about tables inlaid with gold, silver, and ivory; others describe ebony chairs or footstools, inlaid with ivory figures of men and lions. There are even lists of more mundane objects: ladles, boiling pans, and bathtubs. This kind of detail throws some light on the precision of the bureaucracy and conjures a picture of men carrying precious and heavy objects to be checked by the sharp-eyed registrars.

Another category of tablets, dealing with land, contains many texts, but in applying them to an understanding of the Mycenaean economy, the problems are almost as numerous as the tablets themselves.

The land records give the names of people and, often, their occupations, followed by amounts of land and seed. Some of the land is identified by the term *ke-ke-me-na;* the rest is called *ki-ti-me-na.* The two categories seem to be distinct, and the *ke-ke-me na* land seems to have something to do with the *da-mo,* for the tablets say "Pikreus holds a plot of *ke-ke-me-na* land from the *da-mo,*" while the *ki-ti-me-na* land seems to be held from persons. At least, people are similarly named in connection with this category. The appearance of the word *da-mo* occasioned great excitement among the decipherers, as it probably is the Greek word *demos (people,* or *state)* . It has been suggested that this category of land belonged to the people, and that the *demos,* the nonroyal part of the society, had gained some inde-

79

pendence from the king. This is an attempt to see in Mycenaean times the early stirrings of later Greek democracy. Thus the other category of land is taken to have been the property of the king or his retainers, to be parceled out and kept distinct from the people's land.

That there are two separate categories is clear, but to attach to these technical terms broad sociological significance is to ignore some of the essential characteristics of bureaucratic records. These accounts tend to be full of terms which may have had clear and specific meanings only to those who kept the records. With etymologies based on usage of the distant past, even the literal meanings of words may be no clue to their real significance. For example, in Roman Egypt there were many different categories of land, and the titles, like "King's land" (when there was no longer a king), only reflected the usage that had been current before the Romans took over Egypt. So there is great danger in trying to interpret the Mycenaean land system according to the literal meanings of the words used in the records.

It is also necessary to understand the reasons for which the terms were used. One must, as it were, get inside the scribe's head, and try to understand why he bothers to divide land into categories. Perhaps these tablets (which seem to record issues of seed) provided useful information about eventual tax revenue or any kind of income to the palace. It is more likely that *ke-ke-me-na* land of a "public" nature belonged to a separate tax category and that the use of the term bears on taxation, rather than that these terms indicate a real division in Mycenaean society. The word *da-mo* (*public*) may have no more significance than *alienable to any one,* and this land may have had the characteristics of unrestricted right of sale, to be taxed accordingly, while the other land may have had certain restrictions on title or sale that affected its tax liability. Without more evidence than we now have, we cannot give a more precise interpretation of these terms. It remains dangerous to spin elaborate interpretations of Mycenaean society from these texts when it is rather more likely that their significance is narrow, technical, and administrative.

Narrow though the texts may be, they provide an exciting insight into Mycenaean administration. It is clear that affairs had become technical and complex enough to require the creation of separate categories and subdivisions of land and, though interpretation is very difficult, something of the nature of the Mycenaean economy comes through. The society was organized quite carefully and the nature of land tenure was clear—at least to the Mycenaeans. There were established procedures for reporting land, for arranging taxation, and, indeed, for legal alienation. Some of the tablets speak of land "held" by one person for another, suggesting the concept of leasing or renting, and it is likely that the society had established contractual procedures for legalizing these arrangements.

The mere existence of the land lists shows that the central authority at Pylos took cognizance of the negotiations dealing with land. Records were kept not only of those who held some of the *demos* land, but also of each person's holding of another's land. The implication is that the final holder was responsible for the taxes; in any event, it is certain that the palace wanted to know everything about the holding of the land.

The land-holdings recorded in these tablets all seem to have been located near Pylos itself, and probably all the land allotted did not exhaust the arable land available to the Pylians of the capital. Almost nothing is known about land beyond the city. Although the tablets refer frequently to commodities from the towns under palace control, they show no record of the division of the village land. There is some limited evidence, however, that this absence of information is mere accident, and that the palace was as interested in distant land as it was in nearby holdings. One tablet reports that a palace official named Axotas went out into the countryside and examined acreage at the major town of *A-ke-re-wa* and a number of other places, possibly to estimate the loss of crops resulting from some natural disaster, and records his findings.

No one around Pylos could escape the scrutiny of the scribes, and even distant villages underwent examination by touring officials. The area subject to Pylos, extending over a good part of the southwestern Peloponnesus—an area filled with the agricultural and commercial activities of dozens of large and small villages—was elaborately organized for administrative purposes, and all economic activity was controlled from Pylos. At the palace, the flow of information into the central archives was supervised by a bureaucracy which must have been enormous, possibly even by modern standards. The very nature of the records suggests a multitude of harried workers, and more than forty different handwritings have been identified. The tablets themselves, made of that notably impermanent material, unbaked clay, were not intended to record for posterity the glory and wealth of the king of Pylos. They were working records, the receipts and memoranda of current operations, stored as temporary notes to be discarded when the more formal reports were drawn up. Some tablets bring others up to date; some appear to be incomplete, with space left for later entries. The thousand or so tablets from Pylos, covering a very brief period of time, are only a fraction of the records which must have been kept. Some notion of the loss brought by time can be perceived in the records of the much later Roman Imperial period. In the first three hundred years of the empire there were never less than twenty-five Roman legions, and each legion had five thousand men. The legions were paid three times a year, so that there were 375,000 pay vouchers a year. Multiply that by three hundred, and the result is 112.5 million. Of those, only six and a fragment of a seventh survive. That minute survival rate gives some notion of the activity which the thousand tablets of Pylos only suggest.

No authority maintains records for the sake of records alone (although some believe modern bureaucracy has come to that); records are kept to insure that people do what they are ordered,

XXVIII. The archive room at Pylos.

pay what is assessed, and stay where they are assigned. Records are kept to anticipate what can be expected; land lists make tax assessments possible, and tax lists provide a basis for planning income. Records of incoming goods tell the receiver who has or has not paid, and receipts are issued to the payers to protect them from further claims. All this points to a bureaucracy that extends far beyond the record office. It is of little value to know who has not paid his taxes unless there are people available to collect them from those who haven't, so a staff of enforcers is necessary. Furthermore, the existence of a big record office implies the maintainance of a flow of accurate information. There must be people who will insure that what is reported on land lists, for example, is truthful; in other words, there must be inspectors, and the tablet recording Axotas' tour shows that these inspectors did in fact exist.

All in all, the Mycenaean administration of the southwestern Peloponnesus was extremely complex. One central authority used an extensive bureaucracy to control a large area, maintaining a large staff at Pylos and smaller subordinate staffs at each of the major villages. This was no rigidly stratified structure, with each level firmly cut off from the next and tied to the center only by a kind of feudal fealty; rather, a comprehensive supervision controlled all levels, with the central authority reaching directly down to even the lowest rungs. This central administration seems to have exerted a pervasive influence on the lives of the people subject to it.

Social Organization

As the bureaucracy was complex, so too was the society itself highly articulated. One of the most striking items of knowledge provided by the Pylos tablets is the indication of the specialization of labor in Mycenaean times. An extraordinarily large number of crafts is attributed to the people named in the tablets. There are flax-workers, weavers, nurses, reapers, goatherds, shepherds, masons, fire-kindlers, bakers, smiths, spinners, carders, bath attendants, grain measurers, and many others. Some of the tablets even speak of people who are in training for an occupation. The fact that the tablets list the occupations of the people named shows again the care with which this bureaucracy kept its records and, even more important, the multitude of occupations reflects an economic scheme of great sophistication. Only in a wealthy society can so specialized a division of labor subsist. In the Mycenaean economy there was enough economic activity to provide the necessities of life to those whose own occupations were limited to small spheres of work. In other words the economy was so constructed that agricultural produce could pass from farmers and herdsmen to smiths, nurses, weavers, and so forth. It is not known how this was done, although there is some evidence of transfers within the administrative structure to people in the service of the palace. It is easy to understand allotment of food to workers, but the naming of occupations in the land lists suggests that the craftsmen were not all in the employ of the palace. In any case, the great extent of the specialization indicates that the transfer of goods was a

XXIX. Mycenaean bull,
on vase from
Cyprus.

general phenomenon in the society. This probability suggests
the existence of a mercantile class of some sort, but whether the
merchants were only a division of the royal bureaucracy or
whether they were independent and operated for private profit
is not known. A bewilderingly rich array of goods created the
need for the complex economic structure. Besides the ordinary
grain, which should be expected in any economy, there are con-
signments of olives and figs, wine and olive oil. The multitude
of livestock is hinted at by tablets like number Cn131, which
mentions flocks at a place which may be named *Pi-sia:* "from
Pimetas (a man's name), 200 rams, from Kuprios, 50 rams;
from Korunos, 100 rams; from Pleuteus, 90 rams," and so on.
The totals listed on the tablet come to 2137 rams, 135 ewes, and
99 she-goats. Other tablets list oxen, cattle, pigs, and horses.
There are spices to grace the culinary art: coriander and cy-
perus seed, and probably honey. (The tablets at Mycenae list
fennel and sesame seed, safflower, mint, and cumin.)

There are tablets which list items of household use, de-
scribing different kinds of pottery containers and utensils in
great detail. The description of a single footstool—"inlaid with
a man and a horse and an octopus and a griffin in ivory"—
shows how elaborate furniture was. Military equipment, hel-

85

mets, and wheels are listed. Other tablets give accounts of gold and bronze. There are many tablets dealing with unguent oil and lists of spices, fancy furniture, precious metal, and a variety of other goods. All these goods give only a sampling of the economic activity; these are the goods moved or transferred during a very short period of time, and represent just a fraction of the material possessions at Pylos. The economy was clearly able to produce great luxury, and was capable of providing many different commodities in quantity.

All this information comes from Pylos, for no other site has produced a comparable number of texts. The few tablets from Mycenae serve to confirm the Pylos materials, as probably will the texts currently being brought to light at Thebes.

Mycenaean society at Pylos, and almost certainly at every other site, centered on a great palace which administrated many villages sprinkled over a fairly large territory. The administration was of fluid structure, with provincial divisions when necessary, and a number of officials to carry out the business of the realm. The society was most complex: trades and labor had become highly specialized, and the abundant economic activity produced an astoundingly high standard of living, at least for the people of the palace.

All this information was unavailable only fifteen years ago. Until Michael Ventris deciphered the script of the tablets, this knowledge of the Mycenaeans lay veiled from modern men. There is no doubt that more research and further discoveries will bring still more knowledge about the Mycenaeans and about the wealth, the sophistication, and the complex society they built.

CHAPTER FIVE

Early Greek Religion

The Nature of the Evidence

THE STUDY of ancient religion has become almost a discipline in itself. Even the early development of so late a phenomenon as Christianity is not fully understood, and the scholarly literature is filled with disagreements over the most important issues. When men turn to the investigation of the ancient polytheistic religions, the difficulties are enormously compounded. There are no great collections of religious texts comparable to the Hebrew holy books, the Christian gospels, or the accounts of the early Church Fathers. Thus the natures of the ancient religions must be perceived in the implications of works which are, essentially, not theological. This requires interpretation, often of a very subtle sort, and different interpretations of the same works are often made. Yet the students of the religions of historical antiquty have, at least, literary sources to which they can refer; the investigators of Mycenaean religion have not even that. An understanding of Mycenaean religion must be reached in the same way as knowledge about any other aspect of Mycenaean society: through interpretation of the archaeological remains.

If we are to be sure that we are dealing with the religion of the Mycenaeans, we must remove from consideration all the fine female statuettes from Crete, for these may not bear at all on mainland practice. We are then left with only rather schematic representations of individual females from the mainland. These mainland figures were made at a time when fine work could certainly have been done, and the crudity of the work

XXX. Mycenaean figurine.

suggests that they were made for reasons quite different from those for which the Cretan figures were made. The Cretan ladies in their elegant attire, beautifully worked and often painted, were the subjects of considerable effort, while the Mycenaean statuettes reflect only the most rudimentary attempts to delineate the human figure. Therefore, even if the Mycenaean statuettes did have a religious significance, it must have been different from that of the figures from Crete. Then again, the attempt to use these figurines to prove a central "Mother-Goddess" cult completely ignores other evidence from Crete and the mainland. There are statuettes of males from Crete, and some explanation must be made for them. There are figures of animals at Mycenae—are they religious in nature? Any argument which insists on the religiosity of the female figurines must accept the same quality for the others, and any argument which insists upon the identity of the female figures from Crete and Mycenae must accept the identity of all similar figures from both cultures.

Clearly if it is not certain that all the figures are religious in intent, it is better to separate the evidence of the mainland from that of Crete. To pursue knowledge about Mycenaean religion with any safety, all evidence but that from the mainland must be excluded. It is best to start, not from the evidence of art objects, which has preoccupied scholars, but from the only clear and certain evidence about the nature of religion on the mainland.

Gods in the Tablets

Once again the tablets are the key to knowledge. Something of the religion of the Pylians glimmers through a few of the inscriptions, and with startling clarity appear the names of a few of the great divinities of later Greece. Poseidon, the powerful god of the sea, is named again and again, while Zeus, the king of the gods in the later tradition, also is mentioned—as are Hera (the wife of Zeus) and Hermes (the messenger of the gods), along with other divinities not included in the later pantheon.

One large tablet records a series of religious activities. Tn316 reports the bringing of gifts to a number of divinities at various shrines: gold cups and bowls are brought for Poseidon, a "Dove-Goddess" called Iphemedeia, Diwja (the female gender of the name Zeus), Zeus himself, Hera, Hermes, and even the priest of Zeus. The tablet also lists the people assigned to the shrines or to the carrying of the gifts. As a record of the transfer of goods and people to the shrines of the gods, it shows the interest of the palace even in the details of religious observance. Something of the nature of Pylian religion can be perceived in this account. It is clear that the shrines were focal points of worship and, as in all ancient and some modern religions, men showed their devotion by making offerings. Here in the Peloponnesus, as all over the ancient world before and after the second millennium B.C., the faithful sent precious objects to the gods to petition for the fulfillment of their prayers or to protect themselves from divine displeasure. It is exciting to see in this tablet the name of Zeus. This Indo-European deity must have been worshiped from time immemorial; he was known all over the Mediterranean in later centuries and worshiped even before Mycenaean times as far east as India, under the Sanscrit name *Dyaus*.

The other side of the tablet provides more information about the Pylian religion. Gifts are listed here for Potnia, "The Mistress," who appears again and again in other tablets. Other divinities not known in later times also received offerings. A goddess whose name seems to have been Mnasa got a gold bowl, as did Posidaeia (who may be the consort of Poseidon); gods whose names may mean *Thrice-Hero* and *Lord of the House* each got a gold cup. This list is headed by the name of the month, Ploistos, the "sailing month." The divinities are unfamiliar to historians of later times, and even the name of the month passed out of use by the time of later Greek calendars. Even so, they all have linguistic roots meaning something in Greek, and the meanings have religious context.

There is evidence pertaining to religion in other tablets too. Poseidon appears as a recipient of a number of gifts of wheat, and one tablet mentions that his larder was enriched by contributions of cheeses, wine, honey, and cattle. Gifts of olive oil to Poseidon are listed among a series of tablets which include contributions of oil to other divinities as well. There are many contributions to Potnia, and Trisheroes (*Thrice-Hero*) too. If the number of entries is a guide, Poseidon and Potnia were clearly the most important divinities in this part of the Peloponnesus.

The nature of religious observance is also indicated in the tablets to some extent. Offerings to the gods (which were certainly to be expected) were connected with festivals, and rituals performed at certain times. There seems to have been a "Divine Mother," or perhaps more likely a "Mother of the Gods," in one tablet, and her gift of oil was offered at the Festival of New Wine. Scented oil was offered to Poseidon in the month of Pakijanios, and again in the Festival of the Spreading of the Couch. A ceremonial called the "Drawing of the Throne," mentioned in yet another tablet, suggests a public ceremony that involves bringing a divine seat into consecrated grounds or taking it out. Finally, the date of the ceremonies in the big tablet, Tn316, is the month of Ploistos, showing again the calendaric nature of worship. A picture emerges of the Pylians gathering at festivals at certain times of the year, either in Pylos itself or in the surrounding countryside, to celebrate the opening of the new wine and to thank the gods for their gifts. Another festival probably involved a procession behind the god's throne, perhaps as part of a fertility rite. It may even be that the association of divine propitiation in the sailing month of Ploistos suggests a festival, or at least offerings, for the protection of the busy Pylian sailors.

All the evidence shows that the religion of the Pylians was a public one—that is, associated with specific times and places, festivals to which the people could come for sacrifice, gift, and prayer. The fact that the records of religious observance were kept in the palace indicates that religion was intricately tied up with official state functions, and all the evidence of the tablets must be taken to deal with officially endorsed religion.

The devotions centered around certain specific cult places, a characteristic of later Greek religion as well. One well-known such area, *Pa-ki-ja-na,* contained shrines dedicated to at least five divinities: Potnia, Mnasa, Posidaeia, Trisheroes, and the Lord of the House, and other groups of divinities may have had their shrines at other cult areas. This sharing of shrines is found in later Athens in the mutual investment of Athena, Poseidon, and Erechtheus in the Erechtheum on the acropolis, or in the use of the joint temple of Athena and Hephaestus in the lower town. At Eleusis, near Athens, a whole group of deities were served by the cult.

Evidence from Mycenae

Although the tablets at Pylos cast some light on religious practices there, those at Mycenae have no religious import. All the conclusions about religion at Mycenae are drawn from artistic representations turned up by the excavators; without supporting texts, inferences from art become rather speculative. The most famous representation taken to depict divinities is the beautiful ivory group, two women and a boy, found by Professor Wace. The two women sit with their arms entwined,

XXXI. Ivory trio from Mycenae.

and the boy leans over the knee of one and looks at the other. The group is taken to attest to the existence of cults at Mycenae like those of Demeter and Kore at Eleusis, to which the young god Triptolemos was joined to make a triad. This may be, just as the designs of clay seals and the ivory figures of women from Mycenae may depict goddesses and the rude clay statuettes may represent divinities. But it is not necessarily the case, for much of Mycenaean representational art does not deal with divine matters (at least such a connection has never been claimed). Among the ivories there is a head of a warrior and a number of ivory plaques showing sphinxes and griffins, as well as heads of bulls. On a great vase there is a painting of a procession of warriors, and the frescoes in the palaces seem to have no clear relation to divine matters. The magnificent inlaid work on the Mycenae daggers shows, not divine matters, but hunting scenes and running animals. These secular representations suggest that the art which has been taken to be religious may not necessarily be so; in that event, there is no real information about religious cults at Mycenae.

If, however, these statuettes do have a religious meaning, the religion at Mycenae is quite different from that of Pylos. There is no indication whatsoever of the dominant position of Poseidon in the religious lives of the inhabitants of Mycenae, and the only real connection between the two cities would be that Mycenae and Pylos both worshiped a major female deity: the unnamed goddess of the Mycenae figurines perhaps was the Potnia known at Pylos. The divine triad, if that is what the ivory group really represents, has its closest affinities with the later Greek cult near Athens; in this case, Mycenae—like Pylos—exhibits characteristics found in later Greek religion.

That Mycenae and Pylos should be different in religious matters need not be surprising. The individualization of cults among cities was long a characteristic of Greek religion. Not only did each city have its special tutelary deities and its special cults—such as Athena at Athens, Apollo at Delphi, Demeter at Eleusis, and so forth—but even in so small an area as Attica (after it came completely under the control of Athens) the different towns did not all agree on the significance of the same deities.

At Pylos, the group of two women and a child shown in the Mycenae ivory plaque and in the statuettes is rare—if it exists at all. The cults seemed to center about divinities who are presented singly, even if they may share cult places. If indeed the "Two Mistresses and Young Lord" existed at Pylos, the evidence is tenuous and they pale in importance beside Poseidon and Potnia. Poseidon is presented again and again alone, and so is Potnia. Any attempt to link them is an artificial construction;

the Pylians did not see them that way. A demand for an hypothesis despite the present lack of knowledge would force the conclusion that Mycenae and Pylos gave principal importance to different cults.

General Characteristics
of Mainland Religion

The striking characteristic of Mycenaean religion is its resemblance to later Greek worship. Many of the most important Greek divinities appear in the tablets, and the names of those recognized outnumber the names of those hitherto unknown. Even the relationships fits the pattern of later myth; Zeus and Hera, who seem to be worshiped at the same shrine, were married. Iphemedeia, not an important divinity in later times, was said to have been one of Poseidon's brides, and her name at Pylos fits well with Poseidon's dominance there. The characteristic festival orientation of Pylian worship belongs to later observances as well, and the practice of providing gifts to the gods, although not limited to Greece, did later constitute a major part of worship there. Finally, if the interpretation of the worship at Mycenae is not based on a misreading of the archaeological data, as it well might be, even the diversity of cult characteristic of later Greece existed as early as Mycenaean times.

One characteristic of Mycenaean society is suggested by the very lack of evidence: clearly, the society was not theologically oriented. There are no great temples or religious edifices characteristic of a theocratic society. Nothing in the remains indicates much diversion of Mycenaean wealth to the service of the gods, and there are no great temples such as are found in Egypt and the East, nor any parallels to the many sanctuaries on Crete.

The only building which might be a temple is that recently discovered on Kea, the island off the coast of Attica. In one of the buildings excavated, parts of large freestanding female figures were found. There were fifteen to twenty originally, and they ranged up to life-sized in scale. The building clearly served religious purposes; even after the destruction of the site the area of the temple was used as a sacred precinct. The building is unique in the Mycenean, and even Minoan, world, and it is difficult to assess its significance. The statues found within seem to have affinities with Cretan religion, and it may be that further investigation will show that the religion practiced on Kea had no relation at all with mainland religion.

The only structures which can be considered religious are tombs. That there was some kind of cult of the dead seems clear. The early shaft graves were well made, as were the later chamber tombs, and the complex architecture of the *tholos* tombs suggests a real concern that the dead be well housed.

XXXII. Grave stele from Mycenae.

However, the positions of the bodies in the tombs suggest that the religious concepts controlling the treatment of the dead did not demand a permanent veneration of the deceased. Offerings were made at the time of interment, but the skeletal remains of earlier burials were unceremoniously swept aside to make room for the new arrival. It may be that this disregard of bones points to a concern for the dead only so long as the flesh remained. There is at present no way of knowing. So too, speculative but certainly possible is a conclusion that because of the very nature of this cult, the Mycenaeans were receptive of new ways of handling the dead, and for this reason began, toward the end of the period, cremating instead of interring the dead.

A cult of the dead is almost surely only one part of the religion of any people, and the presence of so many gods and activities in the Linear B tablets shows that other side of Mycenaean religion. It is interesting to note that even with the relatively limited expenditure on religion in classical Greece there were magnificent temples and complex religious precincts, while there is nothing at the Mycenaean sites which can be interpreted clearly as a temple. Here and there in the palaces a simple altar stood as a focus of worship, but the gods seem to have received their due in gifts and festivals, not in buildings.

Religion fell under the cognizance of the king. What the gods received, the palace knew. One may imagine that on great festivals the king and the royal family, regally attired and followed by the multitudes of retainers and members of the bureaucracy, came out of the palace into the town for the procession drawing the god's throne among the throngs of worshipers. On the great festival days the king, as representative of the state, may well have performed some of the religious functions himself; in later times the elected public official called "king" served a religious purpose, and the religious character of this vestigial king may well go back to Mycenaean times. The king's scribes kept records of gifts to the gods, but there is nothing to indicate that the religious role of the king was a major part of his activity: the gods had their priests; the king's concern was

XXXIII. Tholos tomb at
Pylos.

primarily secular. The whole society, in fact, must have been
primarily secular.

The very nature of religion will prevent an adequate understanding of Mycenaean religion until and unless more docu-
ments are found to provide evidence. Our limited information
makes it possible to see that some of the classical gods were
worshiped as early as Mycenaean times, while some of the Mycenaean gods seem to have been unknown to later Greeks. We
can see that festivals played an important part in Mycenaean
religion and that the palace was concerned with religious observance and offerings. Perhaps most important, the evidence suggests that religion played no dominant role in Mycenaean life.
To learn more, we must wait for future discoveries.

CHAPTER SIX

The Mycenaeans in Greece

MYCENAEAN CIVILIZATION WAS FAR MORE BROADLY BASED THAN the ruins of Mycenae, Pylos, and a few other great sites would indicate. The palace sites are always first to draw the attention of archaeologists, and the continuing excavations at Mycenae, Thebes, Goulas Island, and Iolkos will undoubtedly bring much interesting material to light. But no idea of the extent of Mycenaean civilization is possible without an account of the numerous settlements scattered thickly all over Greece. Almost everywhere on the mainland there are pieces of Mycenaean pottery lying on the ground or lightly covered by dust—the refuse of centuries. These broken bits of pottery are the clues to ancient towns; they can tell us when the towns were first settled and when they were abandoned.

The Peloponnesus

There were many Mycenaean sites in the area of the Peloponnesus, in which Mycenae itself was located. In this area, the great later city of Argos was settled by Mycenaean times. Nearby at Asine—a town on a hill hard by the coast—another town flourished, while just to the north—at Berbati—was another Mycenaean town. Further east along the coast, the Greeks established a town at the good harbor of Epidaurus, a site already occupied by earlier inhabitants of Greece. Pottery dating back to the Early Helladic period (well before 2000 B.C.) has been found there, and shards of Late Helladic II and III styles show that the Mycenaeans exploited the natural advantages of the site. Nearby, at Areia, there are Late Helladic

XXXIV. Vase from Argos.   XXXV. Attic vase

II and III tombs. Across the Gulf of Argos at Lerna, a site
inhabited since Neolithic times, there are the remains of Late
Helladic I pottery and a Late Helladic II house. Farther north,
above the head of the Gulf, are the sites of Tiryns, Prosymna,
and Dendra. To the northwest, at Nemea, in the lower mountains just off the route from Mycenae to Corinth, there are the
remains of Late Helladic II houses.

All these sites, crowded within a twenty-five mile radius of
Mycenae, have come to light without any special investigation.
Where a careful attempt to discover sites was made in the
southwestern Peloponnesus, along the coast and in the river
valleys, evidence of extremely heavy settlement came forth.
The pottery shows that in some places there was continuous
occupation from the Early Helladic period on, and there are
ninety certain and twenty possible Late Helladic sites of towns
or tombs. The pottery shows that more and more places were
settled throughout the second millennium B.C., and that the
peak of population was probably reached about 1300 B.C., when

settlement in the area must have been very dense indeed. The settlement of the central and southern part of the Peloponnesus, Laconia, was quite similar. Over fifty sites are known, and a number contain the remains of house walls and other evidence of town foundations. Some of these sites had been inhabited since Neolithic times; more commonly, however, settlements began in the Early Helladic period and their number remained about the same until about 1550 B.C. Then, as in the southwest, population rapidly increased, reaching its peak in the middle of the Late Helladic III period, about 1300 B.C.

There were also Mycenaeans living high in the mountains of Arcadia, in the landlocked center of the Peloponnesus, and also in the isthmus around Megara. Corinth was a Mycenaean center then too, and ten sites in the immediate vicinity of that city or along the road leading to Mycenae show that the great strategic and economic value of the land trade routes was well-known in Mycenaean times.

The evidence along the northern shore of the Peloponnesus reveals a somewhat different pattern of occupation. Here, though there are at least sixteen known tomb sites, almost all the pottery is late and ranges from about 1230-1200 B.C. to the so-called sub-Mycenaean styles (about 1060 B.C.). People did not settle down here early to build a long tradition, as they did in the other areas. The Mycenaean occupation came late and suddenly. But in this group of settlements there may have been a heavy population and the evidence in this area, called Achaea, rounds out the picture of a heavy population flourishing at many places all over the Peloponnesus.

Central and North Greece

There were Mycenaeans throughout central Greece, too, as is shown by the evidence at over thirty-five sites. Attica was heavily populated. It is clear that Athens itself was an important Mycenaean town, but the city was rebuilt so often in antiquity that all the buildings of the Bronze Age were cleared away long before archaeologists came to probe the remains. But enough is left to show that the acropolis was as attractive a fortification to the earliest Greeks as it was to those who came later. Greeks began to settle in the Attic countryside, near Athens, in large numbers by about 1550 B.C., and there was a great increase in population in the course of the next two hundred years. In Boeotia there are ten known sites, besides the great fortification of Goulas Island and the palace at Thebes, and settlements flourished on the island of Euboea off the eastern coast.

Farther north, in Thessaly, at least twenty sites have produced Mycenaean remains. In the modern town of Volo (the ancient town of Iolkos), at the head of the Gulf of Volo, three separate sites have yielded Mycenaean materials, and work proceeds apace on the excavation of the palace found there. Late Helladic III pottery abounds at all these sites, indicating that here, too, Mycenaeans thrived. The far western districts of Acarnania and Aetolia were populated, and even far northern Macedonia shows heavy Mycenaean habitation in the Late Helladic period. About half of the thirty known sites there have only Late Helladic I pottery, while most of the rest have yielded both I and III. Although individual characteristics may make definite conclusions risky, the fact that so many sites have nothing later than Late Helladic I makes it appear that in Macedonia, singularly unlike the rest of Greece, Mycenaean activity may have decreased after 1400 B.C.

In every part of Greece where towns flourished in later times, the Mycenaeans preceded their descendants, and the places familiar from later Greek literature were trod by Greeks long before the great writers of Hellenic literature were born. All in all, well over three hundred Mycenaean sites are known, and it is probable that this number would be quadrupled if all Greece were carefully explored for evidence. For instance, there are two hundred place names mentioned in the Pylos tablets for the area around Pylos, but only sixty or seventy sites have been found on the coastal strip in that part of the Peloponnesus. There must have been as many towns in Greece in Mycenaean times as there were five hundred years later—and perhaps even more.

The pottery at all these sites shows that the people living at them were Mycenaeans or shared Mycenaean culture, and—although found at widely separated sites—it is remarkably uniform. From the southwestern tip of the Peloponnesus to the northeastern part of Thessaly the pottery styles were similar. Only the inhabitants of Macedonia created a local style, and even that bears sufficient resemblance to the Mycenaean to show clearly that it was influenced by contemporary styles to the south. This kind of cultural unity—with a *koine,* or com-

XXXVI. Chariot fresco from Tiryns.

mon, tradition of pottery styles—indicates a great amount of intercommunication in Late Helladic times. Not only were there a lot of people inhabiting many cities and towns all over Greece, but they must have traveled a great deal and been in touch with one another.

There were many roads crisscrossing Greece in Mycenaean times, traces of some of which remain. Greek geography is such that Mycenaean traders must have traveled much the same routes as later merchants did. The mountains preclude much freedom of choice, and the few passes through them virtually dictate the paths to be traveled. For example, the road from Corinth down into the Peloponnesus must cut through the mountains along the upland pass past Nemea, and then down into the plain past Mycenae. Some of the Mycenaean towns along this road have been located. Along this and many other routes Mycenaean merchants traveled, probably bringing wheat from the plains of Thessaly and oil from the groves of Attica. It is not yet known whether the Mycenaean towns were interdependent, with Greeks of one place exporting their special products to other towns. The Pylos tablets indicate that all the basic commodities existed at Pylos, but they do not make clear whether all were home-grown or whether some were imported. The presence of so much and such similar Mycenaean pottery from all over Greece can only be accounted for by commercial interchanges. This commerce could have been based on a broadly ranging trade in local products or on the importation of goods from abroad which, in turn, created a flourishing domestic trade. In either case, the relative uniformity of pottery indicates a uniformity of culture.

This culture flowered during a long period of peace. None of the sites shows signs of destruction by war like that which followed the invasions early in the second millennium B.C. This period of peace explains the homogeneity of culture. In a period when cities are not warring with each other, and there is no hatred engendered by the sack and pillage of homes, men can travel freely from place to place and in friendship deal with citizens of far-flung cities. This long era of peace gave the

MAP IV

MYCENAEAN ROADS IN THE ARGOLID

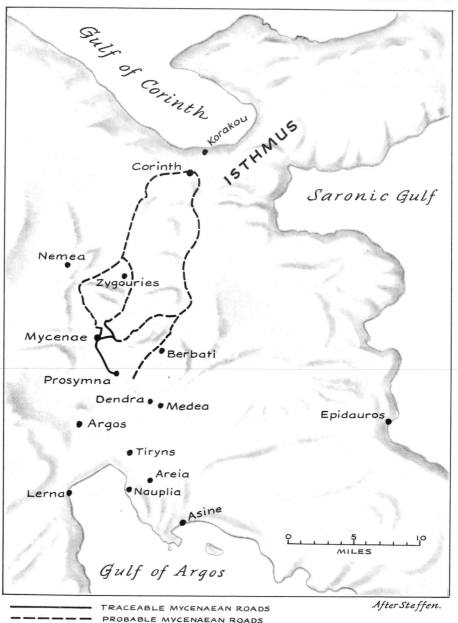

Gulf of Corinth

Korakou

Corinth

ISTHMUS

Saronic Gulf

Nemea

Zygouries

Mycenae

Berbati

Prosymna

Dendra

Medea

Argos

Epidauros

Tiryns

Areia

Lerna

Nauplia

Asine

0 ____ 5 ____ 10
MILES

Gulf of Argos

———————— TRACEABLE MYCENAEAN ROADS

– – – – – – – PROBABLE MYCENAEAN ROADS

After Steffen.

Greeks the chance to develop the vigorous commerce and the cultural unity of the Mycenaean period.

The Mycenaean Greeks penetrated farther north in Europe into areas no longer thought of as Greek. Along the shore of Lake Ochrid, in what is modern Albania, there is a tumulus from which Mycenaean pottery of Late Helladic I type has come. Even if the Greeks themselves did not struggle up the hard mountainous route, their commerce did, reaching into territory which was barely known even a thousand years later. (At the beginning of the twentieth century, a distinguished historian, J. Bury, in the *Encyclopaedia Britannica*, 11th edition [*Albania*], called this area "perhaps the least-known region in Europe.") It is reasonable to believe that a careful investigation of this region and perhaps others even farther north would yield fruitful evidence of Mycenaean activity.

The Power Structure

It has often been said that the Peloponnesus was the center of this far-ranging trade, and that this southern part of Greece was the cradle and heart of the Mycenaean civilization. The statement was inspired by the location of the original discoveries; because these first sites were in the Peloponnesus, scholars assumed that the Mycenaean culture was essentially a Peloponnesian product. Other excavations, like those of Pylos, have tended to confirm the original hypothesis. But, although there is no reason yet to reject the Peloponnesus as a base for Mycenaean power, there is enough evidence of Mycenaean activity over the rest of Greece to make this hypothesis subject to some modification.

The heavy population elsewhere, and the palaces of Boeotia and Thessaly, indicate that if the notion that the Greeks developed their civilization first in the Peloponnesus and then spread it through Greece is true, that development and dissemination must have begun earlier than now supposed. There is enough evidence of Late Helladic I and II pottery in the northeast to indicate that the culture was known there since the beginning of Late Helladic times, and the heavy population growth in Attica and Thessaly, which reached its peak in Late Helladic III, follows the same pattern known in the Peloponnesus. Because the developments in Laconia and in the southwestern Peloponnesus parallel those in the north—not only in population growth, but also in the building of the great palaces at Mycenae, Tiryns, Pylos, Thebes, Goulas Island, and Iolkos—it is clear that civilization in both north and south was advancing in step during the Late Helladic period.

If Greece enjoyed a cultural unity during the Late Helladic period, any export of civilization from the Peloponnesus to the rest of Greece must be placed in Middle Helladic. Even this may not be necessary. People had been living in Greece since Neolithic times, and in some towns had been prosperous almost from earliest times. When the invaders broke into Greece at the end of the Early Helladic period and settled down to live in peace at the beginning of Middle Helladic times (after smashing and pillaging their way across Greece), the cultural change they brought appeared everywhere. It would be perfectly reasonable to believe that there never was an expansion of Mycenaean power from the Peloponnesus to the rest of Greece. The history of these critical centuries of the first half of the second millennium B.C. could well have been one of gradual growth of population and economic activity, with all the centers building wealth and prosperity. By the end of the period all the centers would have been in close connection with each other, an affinity bringing about the wide cultural connections during the Late Helladic "Mycenaean" period.

This is the most economical hypothesis, and would not demand a completely unattested expansion of power to explain the cultural and economic situation in Greece during the Late Helladic period. The history of the second millennium would be one of a large number of people of the same ethnic and linguistic group coming into Greece in about 2000 B.C., and then settling down to live in peace for centuries. This long period of peace produced a prosperity which affected many of the sites, and the inhabitants of all these growing cities shared their discoveries and traded regularly with each other. As their cities grew and the trade routes were more and more heavily traveled, people were encouraged to found new towns to profit by commerce, and this tendency scattered new foundations the length and breadth of the land. The expansion of intercity trade could well have accounted for the homogeneity of Mycenaean culture in the last centuries of the period, and the impetus could have come, not from a drive to the north, but from a general growth all over Greece.

Of course, the explanation that the Mycenaeans created their great civilization with Greece as the sole base is too simple and limited. Greece is not a wealthy country, and it is difficult to see just what even the greatest of these cities might have been able to contribute to make the trade quite so extensive. The catalyst came from outside, and the record of Mycenaean activities outside Greece shows just what did happen. From the southern reaches of Egypt at Aswan all along the Palestinian coast northward to Turkey, along the western shore of Turkey and then across the Mediterranean to Sicily and southern Italy, Mycenaean pottery has rewarded the archaeologists' search. There were imported objects in Mycenaean graves as early as 1550 B.C. This foreign commerce brought the extra benefits with which the Mycenaeans supplemented the available resources of Greece and built a wealthy society.

CHAPTER SEVEN

Traders to the World

The Commerce with Egypt

IN THE middle of the second millennium B.C. the Mediterranean Sea was a busy waterway. Ships plied the coasts of Greece and the Aegean Islands on their way to Palestine and Egypt, carrying the products of workmen in dozens of cities. Some traveled the nine-hundred-mile route to stop at the trading ports of Rhodes and Cyprus on their way to Egypt, while others chose the shorter but more dangerous three-hundred-mile route from Crete to Egypt. There had been contact between Egypt and Crete even before 2000 B.C., but the relations were indirect and did not leave many traces. In the succeeding five hundred years trade quickened and the Minoans of Crete sailed to Egypt and entertained Egyptian visitors at home. Egyptian scarabs of this period have been found on Crete, and an Egyptian statue and an alabastron vase have been found in a Middle Minoan II level of the palace at Knossos. At the same time shards of Minoan vases in styles of this time have been found in Egypt. Although there are not many of these objects, they do show connections between the two societies—either direct or through the intermediary, Syria.

Soon after 1500 B.C. the situation changed drastically. Beginning with the reign of Thutmosis III, an Egyptian king who ruled from 1484 to 1450 B.C., the Egyptians built a strong merchant marine, and in this period of Egyptian maritime power trade flourished and extensive connections with Crete developed. At the same time, Egypt's trade with the Aegean area (as

XXXVII. Gifts from the Aegean to the king of Egypt.

can be inferred from the inscriptions on the walls of Egyptian buildings) underwent a change.

From about 2200 B.C. on, the Egyptians used the term *Keftiu* to refer to some people outside Egypt. Because the pictures of these *Keftiu* which appear on the walls of tombs (along with the name) look like Minoans, *Keftiu* can be securely equated with *Cretans*. The word continued to appear in Egyptian texts all through the Middle Minoan period (2210 to 1600 B.C.) and became much more common between 1500 and 1400 B.C., when many Egyptian objects were imported into Crete. At the same time the Minoans sent exports to Egypt, and there is even evidence of an interplay of artistic influences between the Aegean area and Egypt. Those years when the word *Keftiu* and pictures of them were commonest in Egypt were the years in which the Minoan commerce reached its peak.

The mainlanders too were involved in the Egyptian trade, though not so early as the people from Crete. About the time that Thutmosis began to expand the Egyptian maritime service, a new name appeared in Egyptian texts, which meant *those people who inhabit the isles at the center of the sea*. This might have referred to the Mycenaeans and Cretans together, but the term seems to have become specialized quickly to mean Mycenaeans only. It was at this time that Egyptian imports began to appear on the Greek mainland (they have been found in Late Helladic I and II graves) and Mycenaean products penetrated as far south in Egypt as Thebes and Armant.

With the beginning of Late Helladic III, things changed radically. The name *Keftiu* appeared no more, and only *the people from the isles in the center of the sea* were mentioned in Egyptian texts. This was the time of the great increase of Mycenaean pottery in Egypt. The Mycenaeans were sailing out of the harbors of Greece in force to take up the lucrative trade with Egypt, loading their small boats with precious cargoes to carry off to the distant Nile. The new king of Egypt, Akhnaton, who reigned from 1379 to 1362 B.C., brought changes which made the Egyptians more receptive to foreign influences, and the Greeks took advantage of the new atmosphere. The great quantities of Mycenaean III A wares suggest that the Mycenaeans took the lion's share of the Aegean trade, and this may be partly the result of the destruction of the palace at Knossos on Crete (about 1400 B.C.). Whatever the reason—Akhnaton's accession, the destruction of the palace, or both—there were all kinds of Mycenaean wares in Egypt in the fourteenth century B.C. But the flourishing trade did not maintain its peak: after Akhnaton's death Egypt seems to have been less accessible to the Mycenaeans. Mycenaean III B wares are to be found in Egypt, but not in the same variety as the earlier imports and there is reason to suppose they were made on Cyprus rather than in Greece itself. It may well be that after the beginning of the thirteenth century B.C. the Egyptians were importing only necessities—oil, perhaps—and from Cyprus rather than from Greece. Although we cannot be sure of the reasons, Greek trade with Egypt seems definitely to have contracted.

The Eastern Mediterranean

Fortunately, it was no disaster for the Mycenaean traders, for they had other outlets for their goods. The Mycenaeans had settled in the Aegean Islands and the whole

Levantine coast had been opened up to trade by the enterprising Greek sailors. In expanding commerce, Greek ships had been using many ports either as staging areas for export or as stopovers along the long journey to Egypt. Some of the Mycenaeans settled permanently at a few of these commercial centers, and much of the Mycenaean pottery in Syria and Palestine may have come from these settlements as well as from Greece itself. One of the most important of the overseas settlements was that founded on Rhodes, where vast quantities of Mycenaean pottery on the island remain as a memorial to the early Greek activity there. The change from Cretan to Mycenaean activity in the Mediterranean commerce is signaled by the nature of pottery finds at Trianda, in the northern part of the island. At first only Minoan wares were brought to Rhodes, but as time went on Minoan and Mycenaean pottery was intermixed; finally, Mycenaean styles dominated. The Greeks, coming to Rhodes about 1500 B.C., gradually replaced the Cretan traders. Within a hundred years some had settled in the town of Ialysos, and they spread out from Ialysos all over Rhodes. By about 1250 B.C. the whole island became "Mycenaeanized." The Mycenaeans actually manufactured some of their pottery on the island, and the native islanders, mixing with the new settlers, were making and using Mycenaean pottery at a number of cities and towns.

The Greeks also settled in Cyprus. Apparently they colonized Cyprus a little later than Rhodes, for no Mycenaean I or II pottery has been found there. Some transitional Mycenaean III A:1 vases show that the Greeks were in Cyprus by the end of the fifteenth century B.C., but the style of the next century is much more common. The bulk of that pottery was probably imported by Greeks sailing to Cyprus, although a slight divergence in the style of some pieces indicates that some was manufactured on Cyprus itself. The majority of Mycenaean wares on Cyprus in the next period, 1300 to 1230 B.C., were locally made. As they had done on Rhodes, the Greeks established a colony on Cyprus, and this affected the whole ceramic tradition of the island. (Greek contact with Cyprus had begun a little before 1400 B.C.; in the century after that, the settlements were planted.) By 1300 B.C. the Mycenaeans on Cyprus began to deviate a little from the styles of the Greek mainland, but the pottery styles remained basically Mycenaean.

From these overseas trading posts on Rhodes and Cyprus, Mycenaean traders sailed farther east. The first Mycenaean goods to reach Egypt probably came indirectly, through the great ports along the Syrian and Palestinian coasts. Even when

XXXVIII. Goblet from Ialysos on Rhodes.

the Greeks went to Egypt themselves, they must have stopped off at a number of cities along the coast. The Mycenaeans began to reach the eastern coast of the Mediterranean at about the same time they first came to Cyprus, at the end of the fifteenth century B.C., but only a very few vases earlier than 1400 B.C. have been found.

With the turn of the century, Greek commerce with the East grew rapidly, and there are pieces of Mycenaean III A pottery all along the coast from Tell Atchana in the north to Gerar at the edge of the Sinai Peninsula. Although much of this pottery differs a little from the common types found in the Peloponnesus, its similarity to the styles of Rhodes and Cyprus indicates that the bulk of the trade with the Levantine coast at this time was carried on from the Mycenaean centers on these two islands. Mycenaean III B pottery is found even more frequently than Mycenaean III A, and again much of it suggests Cypriote origin rather than Greek or even Rhodian. At Ras Shamra, a city along the northern part of the coast, so much pottery and so many ritual vessels have been found that there is no doubt that the Mycenaeans established a trading center there, and the III B pottery shows that the settlement came soon after 1300 B.C.

This eastern trade, which burgeoned in the fifteenth and fourteenth centuries B.C., created what might almost be called a Mycenaean trading community. Although the centers at Rhodes and Cyprus accounted for the bulk of the trade with Syria, Palestine, and Egypt, these islands were always closely tied to Greece by bonds of kinship and heavy commercial activity. In good weather, vessels probably plied the seas daily in voyages between Greek ports and the cities of Cyprus and Rhodes, and we may well imagine families spread out about the Mediterranean in pursuit of the profits to be had at sea and abroad. The affinity of the overseas islands to Greece can be noted in the styles of pottery found there. Although there is a "Rhodian ware" and a "Cypriote ware," the difference between these styles and mainland styles is really very slight. The pottery from Rhodes and Cyprus basically belonged to the pottery *koine,* which characterized the unity of all mainland Greece. The permanent residents of the overseas cities introduced some local variation, of course, but the unity of the Mycenaean style endured for a century and a half.

The Western Mediterranean

This same cultural unity is found in the evidence of the Mycenaean penetration in the West, and in this part of the Mediterranean Mycenaean activity began earlier than that in Egypt and the East. Although very little pottery of Late Helladic I and II types is to be found in Egypt, the Levant, Rhodes, or Cyprus, these earliest types of Late Helladic wares are found at Lipari in the Aeolian Islands off the northeastern coast of Sicily, Greeks certainly came to Lipari as early as 1500 B.C., and Middle Helladic pottery at Filucidi, elsewhere on the island, indicates that they were sailing toward the west a hundred or more years earlier. Some Minoans from Crete came too, and left some Late Minoan I pottery to mark their adventurousness, but their trade was subordinate to that of the Mycenaean's. Trade flourished during the fifteenth century B.C., and the Mycenaeans left more and more pottery of transitional Mycenaean I-II ware and then of the Mycenaean II style itself. But, unlike the eastern trade, the peak of commerce in the West came early, and although the volume of III A and B styles matches that of the earlier pottery, there was no great expansion. There is even some Mycenaean III C pottery to show that the commerce lasted well past 1200 B.C.

The accomplishment of the Mycenaeans was no mean feat; sailing across the open sea with heavily laden wooden ships, they pioneered a trade route which was not to be exploited again for many centuries. They opened the way westward even before the Minoans tried the difficult journey, and they so dominated this commerce that at some sites in the Aeolian Islands, as at Filucidi, there is no suggestion of any Cretan presence.

There is less evidence for the early trade on Sicily. There is a vase at Monte Sallina which is probably Middle Helladic, but nothing else earlier than Mycenaean III A. The volume of imports remained constant through Mycenaean III B, when trade seems to have ceased. In Italy, too, the first Mycenaean traders brought III A wares and, interestingly enough, at Scoglio del Tonno in Taranto, Rhodian wares have been found. The earliest pottery there is Mycenaean III A, and this and the III B wares which were found in great quantities show a clear relationship to the favorite shapes and local minor variations in painting styles found at Rhodes. There is also later pottery in significant quantities, and at other sites in southern Italy the III C pottery seems to outnumber the III B, although there is almost no III A. The evidence clearly shows extensive Mycenaean activity in southern Italy and in Sicily during Late Helladic III, and the finds of pottery along the western route from Greece show that the Greeks developed a well-organized commerce during this period.

In the Ionian Islands, directly off the western coast of Greece, the influence of the mainland civilization was felt relatively early. Even before 2000 B.C. the pottery of Ithaca included some styles very similar to those of the mainland. There are pieces of Middle Helladic pottery that resemble those of central Greece and even those of Macedonia. Probably more people lived on this island in Early Helladic times than during the Middle Helladic period or the beginning of the Late Helladic period, and it may well be that the population was severely diminished after the invasions of 2000 B.C. But by the turn of the thirteenth century B.C., the Mycenaeans were re-establishing the relations that had been most vigorous seven hundred years earlier, and after 1300 B.C. Mycenaean pottery became common in the Ionian Islands.

The Middle Helladic pottery in the Ionian Islands and in Italy and Sicily suggests the trade routes chosen by the Greeks in their earliest overseas ventures. They sailed to the islands off the western coast of Greece and then, striking directly across the Adriatic, went on to Italy, Sicily, and the islands off the Sicilian coast. This was the first international venture of the Mycenaean merchants. Later these hardheaded businessmen were distracted from the West by the profits to be made in the East, and there was a great rise in the eastern trade in the latter part of the fifteenth and during the fourteenth centuries B.C. Then, as the eastern trade fell off after 1300 B.C., the Mycenaeans returned to the western routes they had pioneered long before. The whole period of Mycenaean prosperity, marked by the wealth of the sites in Greece and by the rapid rise in population, was the result of wide-ranging international commerce and, for the greater part of this period, the Mycenaeans were the major—if not the only—traders plying the shipping lanes.

XXXIX. Copper ingot from Cyprus.

A Bronze Age Shipwreck

Until recently, most of the evidence about the nature of this trade came from the pottery itself, and the conclusions were generally speculative. There is no way of knowing whether the pottery brought by Mycenaean traders to ports all over the Mediterranean was itself the object of the trade—or, if not, what the pottery might have contained. But new underwater discoveries by archaeologists have yielded some positive information.

About the year 1200 B.C., a ship sank off the coast of Cape Gelidonia in southwestern Turkey. The remains of that ship have been excavated, and the cargo inventoried. The ship carried copper ingots—some shaped like ox hides, others like buns. Piles of tin oxide show that the vessel also carried tin ingots, and there were also many bronze implements. Some of these were broken and, cast in with the copper ingots, were being carried to be melted for reuse. Some of the tools were in good condition, and must have been aboard for the use of the crew; there were whetstones aboard to keep the working tools in good repair.

It is difficult to determine the flag under which the ship was sailing. The wreck was found along the route between Greece and Cyprus, and the Cypriote marks on many of the tools make it almost certain that the cargo had come from the copper mines of Cyprus and was on its way to Greece. But it is not known whether this was a Mycenaean ship returning to Greece, or a Rhodian vessel, or even a Cypriote ship. Nevertheless, we know at least one kind of cargo designated for Greece. The finding of this ship proves what might well be guessed: Greece, poor in metals, imported raw materials to make tools.

The hoard of bronze may also help to supply one answer to the question of the source of Mycenaean wealth. All over the Mediterranean various kinds of swords and daggers have been found in settlements and graves, most of them are types known from excavation sites on mainland Greece. These weapons are artfully and sometimes elegantly made, and some—found in widely scattered places—are so similar that they must have come from the same workshop. It seems almost certain that finished weapons constituted a major export item from Greece. The sunken ship gives an insight into the trade. sailors were bringing the raw copper and tin from Cyprus, and the two metals were to be smelted into bronze and worked into fine products in Greek workshops and then sold aboard.

This ship never completed the voyage, but many others like it must have been more fortunate. Thus Greece in the Mycenaean Age served as one of the earliest industrial centers, importing raw materials for her sophisticated workers to fashion into fine products that would be sold abroad.

XL. Mycenaean swords.

This would have been a lucrative trade, but it is unlikely that it alone could have accounted for Greece's great wealth in this period. The Greeks may also have exported wood to Egypt, as well as anointing oils from the olive trees of the Aegean hillsides. The Egyptians never produced much wood or oil, and a thousand years later the conquering Greeks made a great effort to introduce the cultivation of olive trees into the country. This trade may have brought a sizable income to the Mycenaeans, and could have been accompanied by the transshipment of silver, which did not exist in Egypt and was worth twice as much as gold there. The early Mycenaean trade in the West would have opened up the sources of silver there, and it may well have been the Greeks' discovery of its value in Egypt that first brought them into the eastern trade.

In return for oil and the transshipment of silver, Egypt may have supplied wheat and papyrus to Greece and the West. It is entirely possible that Mycenaean trade consisted largely of transshipment: bottomage is extremely profitable in itself and, primed by the profits of the Mycenaean metal and ceramic crafts, it could account for the wealth of Greece in the Late Bronze Age. The export of oil alone could have brought great profits to Greece, and the olive-growers inland as well as the traders in the ports would have benefited from this trade.

XLI. Daggers and cooking utensils.

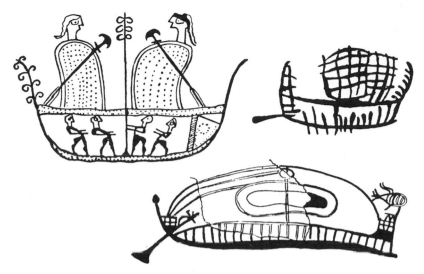

XLII. Drawings of ships, from vases.

The area served by the Mycenaean traders has been called the Mycenaean Empire. This is surely a misnomer, for there is no evidence of Mycenaean domination anywhere. The weapons these men carried brought money, not blood. Prosperity was so great that there was work enough for everyone, and the commerce was so profitable that foreigners could settle alongside native populations without danger and without fighting.

The Greeks, who played such a large part in this commerce, received a correspondingly large share of the prosperity. The trade brought a great increase in the wealth of mainland Greece and probably brought in more food than Greece has ever seen. In peace and prosperity, the population grew rapidly. Mycenaean women calmly watched their husbands sail off on long sea voyages, and the sailors returned with fascinating stories of far-off places. In Egypt artists painted pictures of Greeks on the walls of tombs, and the Greeks probably wove word pictures of the wonders of the pyramids. In this atmosphere Greece achieved its first great flowering of culture, and the whole known world shared in that achievement.

CHAPTER EIGHT

The World of the Mycenaeans

OUT OF THE RUINS OF PALACES AND COLORED BY SCATTERED FRAG-
ments of vases and broken tablets rises a picture of Mycenaean
society, but the ancient dust gives no hint of the grandeur of
the Mycenaean princes or of their importance in the Mediterranean world. When the Greeks sailed to the East, they touched
the ports of powers that were among the mightiest of all antiquity. Just across the Aegean Sea, in what is now Turkey, the
mighty Hittites ruled from the shores of the Aegean across the
mountains into Syria. And far across the Mediterranean lay
Egypt, at the height of its glory, powerful and feared.

Hittite-Egyptian Struggles

The powerful kings of the Egyptian Eighteenth Dynasty began
restoring that great country to native control in the first half of
the sixteenth century B.C. They drove out the nomad Hyksos,
reconquered the northern part of Nubia, and began a successful
campaign to bring Egyptian control to Palestine and Syria. By
the middle of the next century, the great King Thutmosis III
had subjugated Palestine and Syria, and his soldiers stood along
the banks of the Euphrates. These were the years when the
Minoans sailed out from Crete to trade with Egypt, taking advantage of the "Egyptian peace" which Egypt's control of the
Levantine coast had imposed on the eastern Mediterranean.

While Thutmosis III was establishing Egyptian authority in
Syria, a new dynasty was restoring order to the Hittite kingdom
in Anatolia. The Egyptians and Hittites were kept apart for a

century or so by the kingdom of Mitanni in upper Mesopotamia. By the time of King Suppiluliumas who came to the throne about 1380 B.C., the Hittites were ready to contest northern Syria with Mitanni, and under this warrior king they marched down into the plains. The interests of the two great empires clashed as Mitanni, with Egyptian backing, repelled the first Hittite invasion and pushed the invading forces back into the Taurus mountains. But Suppiluliumas, in a second and better-planned invasion, destroyed the capital city of Mitanni, and penetrated as far south as Damascus. In succeeding years, while Egypt was occupied with internal problems, city after city in Syria came under Hittite control. By the time Suppiluliumas died, in 1340 B.C., Egypt had lost her great overseas empire, and the Hittites ruled supreme in western Asia.

But the Hittites were not long to enjoy their triumph. A new dynasty had risen in Egypt and the second king of the line, Sethi I, marched into Palestine and subdued the rebellious princes there, who were supported by the Hittites. As Sethi gained control of Palestine, the Hittite king, Muwatallis, decided to intervene in the Levant. This was the first confrontation of Egyptians and Hittites. In a great battle at Kadesh, about 1300 B.C., the Hittites stopped the Egyptians and prevented their advance into Syria. For a little while thereafter there was peace, with the Hittites holding Syria and the Egyptians in control of Palestine. But in the fifth year of the reign of Sethi's successor, Ramses II, the two armies met again on the same battleground. Although Ramses' monuments in Egypt boast of his great victory, the political structure of the Levant shows that the Egyptian armies were once again repulsed by the Hittites. Muwatallis retained control of Syria; Ramses, of Palestine. This balance held through periods of minor friction between the two states, and an improvement in relations culminated in 1278 B.C. in a treaty of alliance between Ramses II and Hattusilis, Muwatallis' successor. The two kings agreed to forgo aggression forever and to come to each other's aid if attacked. This treaty settled the affairs of the Levant for some

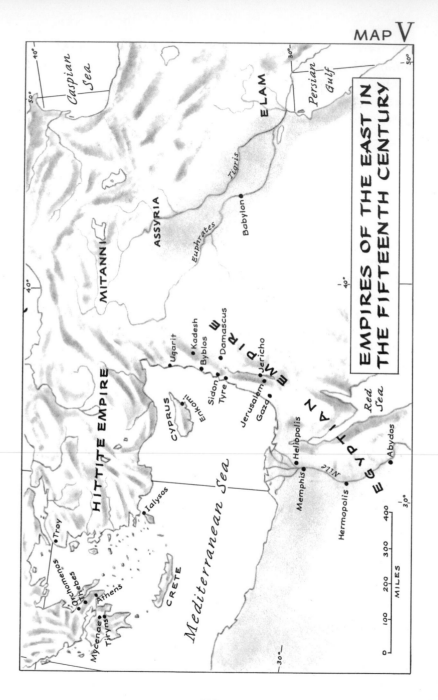

MAP V

EMPIRES OF THE EAST IN
THE FIFTEENTH CENTURY

122

time, and the eastern Mediterranean remained at peace for most of the rest of the thirteenth century B.C.

While the two empires struggled, the Greeks remained on the fringes of the great events that were shaking the world. They had no stake in the East in the sixteenth century B.C., when Thutmosis III was extending Egyptian power over Syria, and even when Mycenaean traders replaced Cretans after 1400 B.C. it was of little consequence to the Greeks whether Hittites or Egyptians controlled the ports of Syria and Palestine. The kings of Greece, far removed from the center of conflict, were secure in their own fortress cities. Their kingdoms were very different from the empires of the East, where vast territories were united under the rule of one all-powerful king. Greece seems to have been broken up into a number of kingdoms—each powerful, but separate and independent of the others. Some of these kingdoms were in northern Greece; others, in the Peloponnesus. And it is rather likely that the extensive trade of Rhodes and Cyprus originated from independent kingdoms on these islands.

The Mycenaeans and the Hittites

Nothing in the Egyptian or Hittite texts indicates that these people knew anything about the structure of Greece or about the details of Mycenaean politics. It is quite clear from the extensive diplomatic records of the Hittite kings that their active international negotiations never reached mainland Greece. There is no mention of any place or people which can be safely connected with Greece, and the Hittite kings seem never to have made alliances with one Greek king against another. If there was any diplomacy practiced in Greece in these times, the Hittite kings had no part in it.

But the Hittites probably did have contact with some Greeks. In the Hittite texts there is a country called *Ahhiyawa* or *Ahhiya,* and the name appears as early as the time of Suppiluliumas, who sent someone into exile there. The country must have been friendly to the Hittites, or Suppiluliumas could hardly have sent an exile there. Later, when the Hittite king, Mursilis II, fell sick at the end of the thirteenth century B.C. Ahhiyawa was still friendly enough to send its gods to effect a cure. At about this time or a little later, a Hittite king sent a long letter to the king of Ahhiyawa, and from this letter comes most of the information about the relations between the two. The Hittite complains about one Tawagalawas (who probably bore some relationship to the king of Ahhiyawa), who wanted to become a Hittite vassal but rejected an emissary as not important enough and then turned to help the Hittites' enemies. The Hittite also complains about the tone that the king of Ahhiyawa used in his letters. But the main issue involves a Hittite subject named Pijamaradus, who had stolen seven thousand Hittite prisoners and gone off to a city called Millawanda. That city was apparently a dependency of Ahhiyawa, for the king of that country—on Hittite request—had ordered his representative there, a man named Atpas, to give up Pijamaradus. When nothing happened, the Hittite had marched into Millawanda at the head of an army, only to find Tawagalawas away, Pijamaradus gone to sea, and Atpas married to Pijamaradus' daughter.

This was essentially where matters stood when the letter was written, and the Hittite king was understandably distressed. He expected no help from Atpas, nor even that Atpas would give the Ahhiyawan king a fair account of the matter, and he complains of an insolent letter from the Ahhiyawan king which forbade him to enter Millawanda. He proposes that Pijamaradus be sent to him and offers a hostage to Ahhiyawa against the latter's safe return. He also asks that Ahhiyawa not be made a base for operations against the Hittites, apologizes for the military occupation of Millawanda, and proposes that the peace between the two countries continue. Apparently peace was kept between the two, for the king of Ahhiyawa sent gifts to Hattusilis in the first half of the thirteenth century B.C.

A number of things can be learned about Hittite geography from this letter. First, it is clear that Millawanda was in Anatolia itself, for the Hittite army was able to march into it. Second, the fact that Pijamaradus was able to escape from Millawanda by sea indicates that it was a coastal city. Finally, it seems clear from the tone of the letter that Ahhiyawa itself was out of reach of the Hittites, or the Hittite king would not have swallowed insult after insult with such patience—mildly remonstrating, meekly asking for a rebellious subject, and even offering a hostage. Hittite power at this time was great enough to reach anywhere in Anatolia: it had kept Egypt out of Syria and crushed rebellions in western Anatolia; any enemies there would had been demolished. But the Hittites never ventured out to sea, and only the sea could have kept their king from marching out to retrieve Pijamaradus as he had marched into Millawanda.

The seafaring character of the Ahhiyawans soon comes to the fore in a treaty between the Hittites and the king of Amurru on the Syrian coast. The treaty contains regulations for commerce with Ahhiyawa, and the scribe—by erasing a passage in which the king of Ahhiyawa is called equal to the Hittite king —unwittingly betrayed the importance of Ahhiyawa and the official policy of the Hittite king as one of not recognizing that importance. There is some indication in this of a cooling off of relations, and this is confirmed in the middle of the century when the Ahhiyawans withdrew from occupied parts of Anatolia at the order of the Hittite king, probably Tudhaliyas IV. During his reign, the Hittites came into direct conflict with Ahhiyawa, first driving a "man of Ahhiya," named Attarisiyas, out of a territory which he had occupied, then defending a place probably in northern Syria against an Ahhiyawan raid. This last mention of Ahhiyawa, as well as the other references to that country, generally show that the nation was powerful, seafaring, and an independent power to be reckoned with by the Hittites. But the texts nowhere make clear who these Ahhiyawans were.

Yet, at that time, the Minoans were finished, the Egyptians had just come out of their cocoon and had been held at the gates of Syria; the only sea power in the eastern Mediterranean was Greece. These were the days of the heavy Mycenaean trade

XLIII. "Warrior" vase from Mycenae.

with Syria and Palestine, when Mycenaean pottery from Rhodes and Cyprus was brought to the Levant and Egypt. There can be no real doubt that *Ahhiyawa* refers to one of the Mycenaean kingdoms. It remains doubtful, however, which of the Mycenaean kingdoms was referred to. All the Mycenaean ships carried Greeks, and the Greeks from all the kingdoms probably spoke the same language, just as they all shared the same culture and carried similar goods. It is not impossible that the Hittites did not discriminate among Greeks and thought them all to be connected with the one place: Ahhiyawa. It is even possible that they did not know of the individual kingdoms in Greece itself. It is reasonable that *Ahhiyawa* referred to a single place and inherently probable that it was one of the Mycenaean centers near the Hittite sphere of influence, perhaps Rhodes or Cyprus.

What is clear is the official contact between the Hittite

kings and some Greek royal house. Even though the Greeks were outside the areas of conflict in the fourteenth and early thirteenth centuries B.C., some of them came into diplomatic contact with one of the struggling powers, and the contact was, for a time, close. The brother of the king of Ahhiyawa visited the Hittite royal house; the Hittite king received gifts from Ahhiyawa and, even when provoked, maintained a friendly and respectful tone. One of the Mycenaean royal houses, though unconcerned with the great events of this time, was enough involved in Eastern affairs to develop a friendship with the Hittites and important enough to become an intimate.

The Hittite texts reveal something which would never have been learned from the archaeology of Greece: the power of international importance, great enough to be recognized by the mightiest empire of the times. We see something of the foreign policy of one of the Mycenaean kingdoms, developing dependencies near Hittite territory and maintaining friendship with the great king to assure itself of freedom to use the ports which he controlled. Emissaries go back and forth; diplomatic correspondence is sent and received; treaties are signed. The Greek kingdom has all the trappings of a respected and recognized power; its king formulates and executes policies of international importance and deals with one of the greatest powers of antiquity.

The Mycenaeans and Egypt

Aegean diplomacy reached Egypt too. When Thutmosis III brought Egyptian forces out of the Nile Valley and back into Palestine and Syria, the Greeks were not long in acknowledging his new conquests. Along with the Minoans, the Mycenaeans came to assure themselves of the friendship of the Pharaoh. On the walls of the tomb of Rechmere, one of the great viziers of Thutmosis III, it is written that "princes of Crete and the Isles in the heart of the sea [the Mycenaean kingdoms] came in peace"; the inscription goes on to say that "they had heard of Thutmosis' victories over all foreign countries, and had brought presents." Though the next words carry the usual Egyptian boast that the princes submitted to the Egyptian king, the fact that they had only "heard of Thutmosis' victories" betrays that these were not conquered subjects bringing gifts, but representatives of independent powers treating with a great king. This diplomatic relationship existed also in the reign of Amenophis IV, at the beginning of the fourteenth century B.C.; but now, with the disappearance of Minoan power, apparently only the Mycenaeans brought gifts to celebrate the anniversary of the king's accession.

Although it is impossible to know which of the Mycenaean kingdoms sent diplomatic representatives to gain access to the Egyptian-dominated ports, there is no doubt that at least some of the embassies came from the Aegean area. Some may have come from Rhodes and even Cyprus, but all, as Greeks, were said by the Egyptians to come from "the Isles in the center of the sea," the maritime Aegean cities of the north. The appearance of these ambassadors in Egypt helps to complete the picture of Mycenaean foreign policy which began to emerge from the Hittite texts. In the fifteenth and fourteenth centuries B.C., Greek kings seem to have had no direct interest in eastern territories, and remained aloof from the struggle for control of the Levant. They were interested only in remaining on good terms with the powers in control of the ports to which they wanted access, and they engaged in regular diplomatic maneuvers in pursuit of that goal. The Mycenaean ships plying the Mediterranean did not come to port by chance; the traders who loaded the ships with goods did not put out to sea in the insouciant hope that somewhere they would find a demand for them and authorities who would let them trade. The traders' way was paved by official visits. Duly authorized representatives of the Greek kings treated with the controlling powers; they set out for Egypt and the Hittite capital in royal vessels, arrived at court with gifts, and were accompanied by all the pomp and ceremony associated with diplomacy. Only after friendly relations had been established between one Greek king or another and his powerful neighbors to the East were negotiations for commercial access concluded.

Of the Mycenaean role in the international structure of the western Mediterranean nothing is known. No civilization in the West had reached the sophistication of the Hittites or the Egyptians, and there are neither records of treaties nor tombs adorned with memorials of gifts and embassies like the tomb of Rechmere. The cities of Sicily and Italy must have seemed crude indeed compared to the elegance of the Egyptian court, but there is no difficulty in assuming that in these lands, too, Mycenaean dignitaries stepped ashore to carry the good wishes of Greek kings.

The Third Force

The realities of the international situation in the Mediterranean more than three thousand years ago are difficult to recreate today. That there were two great land empires in the East is, of course, obvious; the waxing and waning of the power of the Hittite and Egyptian nations has been recorded by their scribes. Though the mighty Egyptians and Hittites clashed, and though their dynasties were sometimes weakened by internal dissension, the completely centralized nature of their dominion over their own and neighboring lands makes their empires understandable to us. But the third great Mediterranean force was different; perhaps just because it was not a single power, it left no record yet discovered that reveals anything of its own view of its role in the Mediterranean area.

But these little Greek and island kingdoms did make up in aggregate a third Mediterranean power, and the respect that the Hittites accorded one of them shows just how important they were. They left their records, not in treaties or on the walls in tombs, but in the objects which their commerce brought to ports all over the Mediterranean. Their royal families dealt with Eastern potentates on an equal basis, but they were not interested in the lands for which so many Egyptians and Hittites died. They were interested in the sea and, after the middle of the fifteenth century B.C., they dominated it for two centuries. They made a third force, and when relations between Hittites and Egyptians shifted from war to peace, and from peace to war, the Mycenaeans kept the struggle from extending overseas, and held the sea lanes open for peaceful commerce.

CHAPTER NINE

The End and the Beginning

ALTHOUGH THE MYCENAEANS' WORLD ROLE LASTED FOR TWO centuries, it finally came to an end. Men whose origins and identities are still mysteries today swept into the area and destroyed the order of the eastern Mediterranean. These marauders are described vaguely in the Egyptian texts as the "Sea Peoples," but the destruction they wreaked was not vague and the change they brought was permanent.

The First Attacks

The first stages of the collapse came in about 1230 B.C., when Pylos was completely overwhelmed. The disaster was so great and the destruction so total that the very memory of the place was obliterated. Not until Professor Blegen's excavations of 1939, four thousand years later, were men to look again on Mycenaean Pylos.

The destruction, though final, was not entirely unexpected. The Pylians knew that something was in the wind, and their last records indicate that they were trying to do something about it. One tablet tells of sending rowers to a place called Pleuron, while another gives detailed descriptions of "how the watchers are guarding the coast." Other tablets list the specific places to which rowers were to go or the names of rowers absent. All this hints of military dispositions, and the specific mention of guarding the coast shows that for once Mycenaeans feared danger from the sea. But all the precautions were in vain. Whoever it was that the Pylians were guarding against penetrated the defenses and destroyed the site, leaving behind nothing but ashes.

Pylos was not the only center to suffer. Thebes, Iolkos, Goulas Island, and Tiryns which, along with Mycenae and Athens, had been building fortifications during the III B period, were no more successful in prolonging their existence than was the unprotected Pylos. Around 1230 B.C. habitation at these sites ceased. At Mycenae the people withdrew into the citadel area and extended the protective walls to include the water supply. The Athenians did the same, and both cities survived the tide of destruction, though at Mycenae some of the houses outside the walls were burned. Even smaller settlements—such as Zygouries, Prosymna, and Aegina—were abandoned at this time, showing how general the disturbances were.

The Attempt to Survive

The pressure was great, but Mycenaean civilization was so strong that it was almost able to survive it. Life went on at Mycenae for a hundred years, and in this period the Mycenaean artists created still new pottery styles: the so-called "granary style," geometric painting in banded designs, and the "close style," a showy, figured painting covering the whole surface of the vases. Other cities—Athens, for instance—survived the onslaughts, and most of the settlements in the Aegean Islands were untouched. In general, although some of the greatest cities went up in flames, the Mycenaeans clung to their civilization and managed to preserve it in most of the areas they had settled.

Nevertheless, the entire Mycenaean world showed the effects of the great upheaval. Overseas sites, such as Ras Shamra and Cyprus, seem no longer to have had the close connection with mainland Greece they had enjoyed in the previous century. At Cyprus, which had suffered one destruction roughly contemporary with that of Greece, and then a second soon after, people grimly continued their lives though severed from the mainland. During the previous centuries, although the Cypriotes had

XLIV. Fragment of late vase from Mycenae.

maintained a native style of pottery, Mycenaean pottery was made on the island and showed a very close connection to that of Greece. By the twelfth century B.C., the situation had changed entirely: the native pottery had merged with the Mycenaean to create a style clearly based on the Mycenaean, though quite different from III C styles found elsewhere. This probably resulted from the influence of large numbers of Mycenaeans who had settled on the island during the III B period, possibly reinforced by immigrants who came from Greece after the disasters there. The newcomers so outnumbered the native Cypriotes during the III C period that, though cut off from Greece, they introduced a culture which, in spite of strong local variations, was essentially and originally Mycenaean.

The increased local differentiation in pottery styles was

significant for Greek history. The flourishing trade which had helped the Mycenaeans rise to their greatness was suffering from foreign interference. The constriction of trade was probably one of the reasons for the settlement of new areas by the Mycenaeans: the traders must have been seeking new bases for the continuation of their prosperity. The strength and drive of these people did not permit them to retire behind their walls in despair; once the impact of the destructions had passed, new settlements were formed in other parts of Greece. Now Achaea comes to the fore, and in this area along the northwestern coast of the Peloponnesus there is evidence of the Mycenaeans' move westward. From tombs comes pottery of the imaginative "close style," though the patterns here are much more subdued than those at Mycenae; the "granary style" which dominates the wares of Achaea is the same as that of Mycenae. The styles are local though, as those of Cyprus were, and this shows that the once-constant contact between the communities was not restored. The attempt to create a new trading community seems to have failed, and the province became isolated. The settlement persisted for a long time, however, from ca. 1230 B.C. to at least 1050 B.C., but finally just dwindled away in the first decades of the first millennium B.C.

This effort to move west brought the Mycenaean III pottery to Sicily and Italy. Although the signs of contact between Sicily and the Aegean are not pronounced, they do exist; Italy, with some very late III C pottery around Taranto, shows an even stronger connection throughout the period. But in spite of the continued contact, the local style developed is more similar to those of Kephallenia, the Ionian Islands, and western Greece. The pottery of the Ionian Islands, in turn, provides the closest parallel to that of Achaea. This configuration of influences demonstrates the purpose of the Mycenaean settlements in Achaea and helps to delineate the nature of the commerce after the thirteenth-century destructions. It appears that the Mycenaeans tried to open new routes of trade through Achaea, the Ionian Islands, and westward, but that the attempt to find a new commercial basis for the old prosperity never quite suc-

XLV. Vase from Cyprus.

ceeded. The settlements were successful and there was trade between the western Peloponnesus and Italy, but not in great quantities, and the connections between them were not strong enough to prevent much local differentiation.

Developments in the East were very similar. A distinctive local style evolved on the island of Cyprus, but at the few places further east where there is evidence of Mycenaean influence the localization is even stronger. Along the Levantine coast there are no strictly Mycenaean imports, although the native pottery retained some aspects of the earlier Mycenaean styles. There is a true Mycenaean local ware at Tarsus on the northern shore of the Mediterranean, but in general there is little evidence of trade anywhere in the East. Only at Rhodes does there appear any strong evidence of connections with mainland Greece.

Two things are clear from all this evidence: at the end of the thirteenth century B.C. something happened in Greece which shook, but did not shatter, Mycenaean civilization. Wealth and population shrank, but the culture did go on and, in a few places, quite successfully. The events in Greece were accompanied by changes abroad which severed connections between Greece and almost all of the East, and left even thriving centers isolated from each other. It is safe to say that nothing was left to the Greeks of their productive eastern trade. The disruption of foreign trade did not extend so seriously to the commerce with the West, but nothing could compensate for the loss. Western trade was limited and apparently moved through intermediaries. Thus the Greeks on the mainland, shaken by events, cut off from the East and only haltingly moving toward the West, faced a difficult future.

The Mysterious Sea People

The extent and violence of the change which had come over the world is the more puzzling for the obscurity of its causes. Egyptian records tell of the overturning of the Hittite Empire by a confederation of Philistines, Tjeker, Shekelesh, Denyon, and Weshesh. "No land could stand before their arms," says Ramses III at the beginning of the twelfth century B.C. (though he goes on to boast that he stopped them at the gates of Egypt). These people, or some of them, had fought against Egyptians in the previous century as mercenaries of the Hittites, and the Egyptians had known of them then. The alliance between the Hittites and the Egyptians may have been prompted in part by the desire for protection against the forays of some of these people. Nevertheless, the Hittites were smashed, and the marauders were barely kept out of the land of the Nile. Some of these people may have been from places settled by the Mycenaeans. The Denyon may have been Danaoi, the Homeric name for *Greeks*; the Shekelesh may have been from Sicily; the Sherden may have been Sardinians. This general Mediterranean upheaval may have been associated with the trouble the Hittites had been having with the Ahhiyawa just a short time earlier, and these troubles may have been forebodings of the destruction of that great empire. Although Ramses III was able to repel the invasion, the general disruption engendered by the attack so weakened Egypt that the feeble kings who followed Ramses were unable to assert their control even over their own country.

All these disturbances struck the eastern Mediterranean during the century before 1100 B.C. The "Sea Peoples" who had been repulsed by Ramses III were not destroyed, nor was their mission entirely a failure: they completely shut off Egypt from the commerce which had flourished throughout the eastern Mediterranean, and many of them settled along the Levantine coast. The Philistines took the coast of Palestine, and older inhabitants like the Phoenicians became independent when foreign power receded from the Levant. Throughout the East the political structure built up by the Hittite and Egyptian kings was undergoing change. The effect of all this on the Mycenaeans was profound. Their commerce in the East was ended, and it is likely that the destruction on mainland Greece was perpetrated by the same "Sea Peoples" who destroyed the Hittites and almost took Egypt.

Knowledge of these events is so limited that only a hypothesis exists to explain the turmoil of this period. This hypothesis suggests that when the "Sea Peoples" began their movements around the Mediterranean at the end of the thirteenth century, among their victims in a series of piratical raids were many Mycenaean sites. The impact of the hit-and-run raids had the immediate effect of driving some of the Mycenaeans, like those at Athens and Mycenae itself, back behind their own walls for safety, while at other sites raids brought complete destruction and the end of habitation. After the raids passed through Greece, some of the Mycenaeans rebuilt and tried to carry on the earlier civilization. Many individuals, and perhaps whole families and tribes, with cities and homes leveled and nothing in Greece to keep them, may have gone on with the "Sea Peoples" to continue the raiding further east.

Certainly it does seem that it was primarily the eastern Mediterranean that was under onslaught in the twelfth century B.C. It was, after all, to the West that the Greeks turned when they were attempting to open up new trade routes, and the new settlements in the northwestern Peloponnesus and the continued prosperity of the settlements of the Ionian Islands and

Italy make it appear that there was still some safety there. In the East, however, the Greeks were cut off from their compatriots on Cyprus and Tarsus, who went on to develop their own local cultures. The closing of the trade routes to the East after the disasters at the end of the thirteenth century suggest that the principal theater of hostilities was the eastern Mediterranean.

Certain facts can be stated with conviction: many Mycenaean centers were destroyed at the end of the thirteenth century B.C.; the Hittite Empire was destroyed at the beginning of the twelfth century B.C. and the conquerers were barely repelled from Egypt; new people settled in the eastern Mediterranean in the course of the twelfth century; Mycenaean trade was cut off from the East and turned to the West. All these events dealt a serious blow to the economic basis of Mycenaean prosperity, and the constriction of trade together with the devastation of Greece must have brought a significant drop in the population of Greece. But Mycenaean civilization managed to survive, not only in the settlement of new communities but in the preservation of a few of the old great cities.

XLVI. Mycenae. Secret stairway to cistern.

The walls of Mycenae, built during the fourteenth century B.C., held the raiders out of the acropolis, but some houses outside the fortifications were burned and never reoccupied. Life went on inside the citadel, and in all probability the complex society of earlier times continued, albeit on a reduced scale. Precautions were taken for the future: the walls at the eastern end of the acropolis were extended to include a secret stairway leading to a cistern, thus assuring the safety of the water supply in the event of future trouble. At the same time, a back gate was included in the new walls to provide access to and from the citadel. Buildings as well as walls were erected during this century, and the elaborate "close-style" pottery found in Mycenae attests to the continued vigor of the artists in the city. The new construction and the continued artistic activity suggest a general optimism about the future.

The End of a Society

Nevertheless, the civilization at Mycenae was doomed. Perhaps a hundred years after the first attack came another which completely razed the citadel. All over the acropolis, the last of the III C pottery is covered by a layer of ashes. For all intents and purposes habitation ceased; although a few squatters may have remained in the ruins of the city, they left no traces. Only much later, with the erection of a temple and sanctuary, is there any indication of reoccupation.

Elsewhere the end was not so grim and bloody. The settlements of Achaea, founded to bring back prosperity to the remaining sites of the Peloponnesus after the thirteenth-century raids, outlived their founders until well after the destruction of Mycenae. In Achaea the local style of III C pottery continued and, as time went on, it foreshadowed later Greek geometric style—examples of which, dated about 900 B.C., have turned up there. Mycenaean pottery of very late style lasts almost until the time of the earliest geometric of the area, and may in some instances be as late as 1000 B.C. This very late date would still leave a gap between Mycenaean habitation and the later

XLVII. Postern gate fortification.

occupation, but it must be remembered that all the pottery from Achaea comes from tombs there. There are no habitation sites with strata to provide information about developments in the area, and we must admit the possibility that excavation of a site would show continuous levels of occupation. The evidence suggests a withdrawal of population about 1000 B.C.—but not as the result of hostile action, as at Mycenae. Instead, there seems to have been a decrease in population through the eleventh century B.C., until community after community dwindled away. It is perfectly reasonable that this should have been the case. These settlements were formed in response to the need of the cities of the eastern Peloponnesus to find new trade routes to the West; once the original centers were destroyed, there was no real economic basis for the Achaean communities. Thus, without a reason for their existence and isolated from the rest of Greece where new life was stirring, they died a quiet and unnoticed death.

This peaceful demise is the most interesting aspect of these settlements. It shows that the disaster which overtook Mycenae did not result in a general destruction of Mycenaean civilization all over Greece. The history of the century after the first raids indicates that the shaken civilization did collapse after another series of raids, but not all places in Greece were struck by hostile action. Most sites were left unoccupied after the end of the III B period; more were abandoned about 1100 B.C., the end of the III C period; and all but a few final survivors disappeared in subsequent years. There may have been no disturbance at all at the small site of Asine on the Gulf of Argos in the eastern Peloponnesus, and at neighboring Argos it is almost certain that nothing occurred to interrupt the continuity of oc cupation. It is from these tenaciously occupied towns that we have a picture of the real end of the first great Greek civilization.

Transition at Athens

But something did remain: the indomitable will of the Greeks to hold on to something of the glorious past. One area of Greece seems to have been left with a sizable population even after the wave of terror. In Attica, although there was some reduction in population, the drop was not comparable to that over the rest of Greece; indeed, some of those uprooted from their homes elsewhere may have come to settle there. Whatever the reason, the people were there, and they left a record of their lives even after the end of the Mycenaean period.

Much of the evidence comes from graves, and some of the material—notably from a cemetery in the potters' quarter of Athens (the Kerameikos) and from some graves on the island of Salamis—has long been known. Scholars examining the pottery from these graves have classified the various styles. The chief style of the period, fully developed a few hundred years after the collapse of Mycenaean civilization, is the geometric, with carefully organized linear patterns. The style developed naturally from the so-called sub-Mycenaean, based on the Mycenaean styles that had evolved before the disasters. The sub-Mycenaean style grew into the protogeometric, the immediate ancestor of the high geometric style.

In Attica the sub-Mycenaean period probably began toward the end of the twelfth century B.C. The Mycenaean occupation of Attica had been heavy, and the acropolis at Athens had a palace like the other great Mycenaean cities. Athens had much the same experience as Mycenae during the disturbances, and there too some houses outside the walls were burned at the end of III B (about 1230 B.C.) and had been abandoned. The later pottery shows the influence of the close style of Mycenae, and much is of the granary style. The great difference between Athens and Mycenae was the continued inhabitation of Athens, and the graves of those who died after the great upheaval in Greece provide an index to the changing and developing culture. The earliest clearly non-Mycenaean burials are very simple; the dead, many without gifts, are laid in rectangular pits. Most of the metal found there is bronze, though there is at least one grave with gold. The pottery shows its inheritance from Mycenaean times: many of the vases are almost completely encircled by black bands, with concentric half-circles on the shoulders; others, lighter in appearance, have open areas between the bands, which are taken up by wavy lines, and the same hand-drawn circles on the shoulders. These motifs are clearly derived from Mycenaean styles, and the extensive banding is a direct inheritance from the granary style. Although the simplicity of the burials belongs to a culture much poorer than the Mycenaean, the continuity of decorative style shows that the Athenians were direct descendants of the earlier Greeks and heirs to the Mycenaean civilization.

Unfortunately, very little is known about the people who survived to 1100-1050 B.C., whether in Attica or in the rest of Greece. There is very little evidence about the connections between people in the different parts of Greece, and there was

XLVIII. Sub-Mycenaean vase.

probably little communication among them. People probably stayed close to home, huddled in the surviving communities, fearful of the hostile world outside the gates. Their recent experiences were not conducive to any feelings of security. In the north, continuity from Mycenaean times was broken in Thessaly, which in the eleventh century B.C. had little connection with southern Greece and had its closest affinities with Macedonia. But at one Thessalian site, Theotokou, excavators of a tomb produced a vase of definite late Attic sub-Mycenaean type, and some jewelry so similar to the Attic that it might just as well have come from an Athenian tomb. So, by 1025 B.C., some connections between Attica and the north had been established, however slight and tenuous they might have been. And across the Aegean, out of a tomb at Assarlik in Caria came a vase strongly resembling Attic sub-Mycenaean or early protogeometric. Thus it is clear that, by the end of the sub-Mycenaean period, the Greeks in Attica were reaching out from the

XLIX. Protogeometric vase.

isolation which the disaster of the preceding century had imposed upon them; traders were probably setting out over the roads leading north, and merchants were launching ships again. In the same way, the inhabitants of the remaining settlements on the island of Kephallenia managed, in the sub-Mycenaean period, to re-establish some communication with northern Greece.

The Beginnings of Hellenic Civilization

The outward expansion characteristic of the Mycenaean period was beginning to reassert itself. Men were recovering and re-exploring the world again. Attica was reawakening and many great changes were taking place. The cemetery on Salamis Island, with its multitude of sub-Mycenaean burials, was abandoned. At Perati, a coastal town which had been a flourishing community in the III C period, a scattering of sub-Mycenaean remains indicates that the inhabitants abandoned the community peacefully at about this time to move elsewhere. They must have gone to Athens, where the settlement seems to have been heavier at the time when the new protogeometric pottery replaced the sub-Mycenaean style. This new pottery had its roots in the Mycenaean past, just as its predecessor did, but it was quite different. The finishes were lustrous, not dull, and bands of paint emphasized the structural shapes of the vases. In many cases lighter decoration was used, with fewer and narrower bands marking off the feet and necks of the vessels. Often, in large closed-neck jars (amphoras) the belly was left completely blank, or had more open decorations. The wavy lines of past styles reappear with greater vivacity, drawn freehand on a white background, and the freehand concentric circles of sub-Mycenaean vases become more rigid and are drawn with multiple brushes. The new vases were better organized in their decoration and the clay was of finer texture. Even the shapes which the potters devised were slimmer in appearance. A whole new style of painting and a fresh concept of the appropriate and desirable mark the resurgent Greek artistic impulse.

The revival must have begun by the end of the eleventh century B.C. The new pottery and denser population at Athens are marks of renewed vigor, and the abandonment of the towns in Attica suggests that the population of the area was being gathered into the city. This may have been the natural outcome of attraction of the one remaining large center. Or, Athens herself might have brought about the change, making the surrounding villages subjects and possibly even forcing some of the inhabitants to move to the city. Both suggestions are entirely speculative, but the fact remains that Athens grew while the surrounding area was slowly depopulated. Whatever the explanation, not many people need have been involved. Some of the sub-Mycenaean evidence could have been left by hamlets of only twenty or thirty families, and it does not take much activity to entice away the entire population of a settlement of that size. So at the time of the new pottery style, an indication of renewed vigor and experiment, the city of Athens was growing stronger as the political corollary of the resurgent Greek culture. But even in the new growth, the elements of past culture persisted, and the men of the new era never completely lost their ties with their great forefathers. Some of the new elements grew out of styles descended from Mycenaean times; others derived from even earlier patterns.

A new day was dawning all over Greece. Thessaly, which had been an integral part of the Mycenaean area, sharply broke with its past and came under the influence of Macedonia, where there had been less Mycenaean influence and which changed little after the eleventh century B.C. The Peloponnesus seems to have had little life during the period of the first developments at Athens, while in the West the earlier culture went on without a break. But as protogeometric pottery appeared in Attica, a cultural revival on a broader scale, rising from the negligible traces of sub-Mycenaean elements, was taking place elsewhere. In the Argolid, wherever men continued to live after the twelfth century B.C., sub-Mycenaean styles gave way to protogeometric styles similar to the Attic, but distinctly local. Throughout Laconia, which had been nearly empty in the years immediately after the fall of Mycenae, protogeometric pottery turns up. Although the quantities are not great, they are enough to trace the resumption of inhabitation. Even as far west as Italy, the late Mycenaean styles developed into a local version of protogeometric.

With no sites of the period excavated, it is very difficult to know much about the century after the fall of the Mycenaean civilization. Nothing remains to indicate the kind of towns or houses people lived in, or how they carried on their daily lives. There are no hints about the political structure or the economic life of Greece in those days, and even the painful piecing together of the fragmentary information provided by the Mycenaean tablets is impossible without some texts. A new kind of writing eventually came into Greece, but it is not known whether it developed in an area which had lost the art of writing, or whether Linear B survived in Athens, for example, to be replaced by a better script. The little that is known of the period has been learned in Attica, and particularly at Athens, but even the evidence there does not reveal whether the community had slumped into a semibarbarous state, or whether it maintained some of the old, sophisticated patterns. The succession of styles at Athens might indicate that the city was the fountainhead of the protogeometric style all over Greece, but protogeometric pottery at sites of continuous habitation in the Argolid and as far west as Italy is an argument against attributing all the cultural impetus to Attica. But it is also difficult to avoid attributing a significant role to Athens. The tenuous connections between Athens and the rest of the Greek world show that the Athenians, even as early as the sub-Mycenaean period, were moving out again to explore the world, and were in the forefront of the restoration of some kind of communications in the Aegean.

So Greece was stirring again. Just as the great wave of destruction in 1230 B.C. could not completely destroy what the Mycenaeans had built, so the final collapse of the Mycenaeans did not spell an end to the Greek adventure. Although the formerly prosperous and populous Peloponnesus was now settled in only a very few places, although northern Greece was isolated from the south and the west almost completely cut off, Attica managed to go on and to create something new out of the old. By 1000 B.C. new life was springing all over Greece; the scattered traces left behind provide hints of the brightness of the hopes in that new era.

Bibliography

THE FOLLOWING BOOKS—A SELECTION OF GENERAL BOOKS DEAL-
ing with Mycenaean civilization and related subjects—are listed
in reverse order of publication, most recent books first. More
specialized and detailed bibliographies are furnished by some
of the books listed below, and these are so indicated. In addition, a periodical bibliography is published, under the name
Nestor, edited by Emmett L. Bennett, Jr., by the Institute For
Research In The Humanities, The University of Wisconsin,
Madison, Wisconsin.

The Cambridge Ancient History, Volumes I and II (New Edition)
Cambridge University Press, Cambridge

This multivolume series provides an exhaustive connected history
of the ancient world from the beginnings of civilization to the end
of the Roman Empire. Each volume contains essays by specialists
in specific fields. The first two volumes are now in the process of re-
vision and reissue, and it is these volumes which contain information about Mycenaean and contemporary civilizations. At present,
each chapter is issued as an independent booklet, under its own
title and author. The chapters contain up-to-date summaries of what
is known about the different aspects of early civilization and,
although they are often technical and not intended for the non-
specialist reader, they are comprehensive and contain full bibliographies.

Greece in the Bronze Age, Emily Vermeule
University of Chicago Press, Chicago, 1964

This comprehensive survey of early Greece, from the beginnings
of settlement to the end of Mycenaean civilization, presents more

information than any other single book. Although the reader without training in the field may find the treatments of some subjects technical, he will also find a full account of the archaeological evidence, some interpretation, and a valuable bibliography, by subject, to lead him to sources of further information.

The Mycenaeans, Lord William Taylour
[Ancient Peoples and Places 39] Thames and Hudson, London, 1964

Intended more for the general reader than *Greece in the Bronze Age,* and much smaller in compass than that book, this provides an introduction to Mycenaean culture. Much of the discussion deals with the material aspects of Bronze Age Greece, but attention is paid to an examination of what can be known about Mycenaean life and history.

From the Silent Earth, Joseph Alsop
Harper & Row, New York, 1964

This book is primarily an account of the excavations of Pylos, written by a prominent American political reporter. The author interprets the significance of the finds at Pylos, and turns his political experience to advantage in an attempt to place our knowledge of the Mycenaean world in a framework of an international power structure.

Troy and the Trojans, Carl W. Blegen
[Ancient Peoples and Places 32] Thames and Hudson, London, 1963

This examination of the development of the civilization of Bronze Age Troy is written by the director of the modern excavations of Troy. It presents to the general reader the results of many seasons of excavation, reporting the significant finds and the important evidence for the different periods of Trojan history, carefully deducing what may safely be said about the culture at each stage of its development.

Mycenaeans and Minoans, Leonard R. Palmer
Alfred A. Knopf, New York, 1963

This book presents the author's interpretation of the evidence of the Linear B tablets. Although other evidence is taken into account, primacy is given to the explication of the contents of the tablets and what they show about Mycenaean society. There is a serious attempt to examine the Linear B tablets from Knossos in order to understand the relationship between Mainland Greece and Crete, and in this study the author proposes a new chronology for the tablets on Crete.

The Hittites, O. R. Gurney
Penguin Books, Baltimore, Maryland, 1962

This is more a history than an archaeological survey. The author presents an outline of Hittite history, and accounts of various aspects of Hittite civilization. Both archaeological and written evidence is used, and a clear picture of Hittite culture and its role in the world emerges.

Prehistoric Crete, R. W. Hutchinson
Penguin Books, Baltimore, Maryland, 1962

The author of this book traces the development of the civilization of Crete period by period, and discusses the material remains found by the excavators. The book contains a comprehensive account of the finds, and although the account is primarily that of the growth of the material culture, attention is paid to developing a picture of the nature of Minoan society.

Crete and Mycenae, Sp. Marinatos and Max Hirmer
H. N. Abrams, New York, 1960

This book is essentially a collection of photographs, and presents, through the fine work of Max Hirmer, a visual account of Mycenaean and Minoan objects and ruins. An explanatory text is provided by Sp. Marinatos.

History and the Homeric Iliad, Denys Page
[Sather Classical Lectures] The University of California Press, Berkeley, 1959

This book provides an introduction to the study of Homer through historical techniques. It marshals information bearing on Homer, and discusses the authorship of the poems. It is useful to the study of Mycenaean history primarily for its first chapter, which provides an excellent synthesis of what is known about the relations between the Hittites and the Greek world.

Ancient Mycenae, George Mylonas
Princeton University Press, Princeton, New Jersey, 1957

This work deals with the single city of Mycenae. It tells what is known about the city in the Bronze Age from archaeology, attempts to relate that information to legends about early Mycenae, and provides a full account of the recent discoveries in Grave Circle B made by the author.

Index

Index

Arabic numerals refer to pages, Roman numerals to illustrations; maps and plans are specified.

157

TWENTIETH CENTURY VIEWS

Forthcoming Titles

D